People to Know

Willa Cather
Writer of the Prairie

Sara McIntosh Wooten

Enslow Publishers, Inc.

44 Fadem Road · PO Box 38
Box 699 · Aldershot
Springfield, NJ 07081 · Hants GU12 6BP
USA · UK

Acknowledgments

The author wishes to thank Patricia K. Phillips and Vicki Bush of the Willa Cather Pioneer Memorial and Educational Foundation, Red Cloud, Nebraska, for their patient assistance in helping me understand Willa Cather and her world; Katherine Wyatt and Chad Wall of the Nebraska State Historical Society, Lincoln, Nebraska, for their invaluable assistance in obtaining Cather pictures; Jenni Kim for providing helpful information about the American Academy of Arts and Letters; Sister Joseph Adele Edwards of Mount St. Mary's College, Los Angeles, California, and Robert Thacker of St. Lawrence University, Canton, New York, for reviewing the manuscript; Nina Rosenstein, whose suggestions brought words to life; and Bob and Jean McIntosh for their unfailing faith and encouragement.

Library of Congress Cataloging-in-Publication Data

Wooten, Sara McIntosh
    Willa Cather : Writer of the prairie / Sara McIntosh Wooten.
        p.   cm. — (People to know)
    Includes bibliographical references and index.
    Summary: Describes the life, career, and writings of the Pulitzer Prize winner who immortalized the Great Plains and Nebraska countryside.
    ISBN 0-89490-980-0
    1. Cather, Willa, 1873–1947—Juvenile literature. 2. Women novelists, American—20th century—Biography—Juvenile literature. [1. Cather, Willa, 1873–1947. 2. Authors, American. 3. Women—Biography.] I. Title. II. Series.
PS3505.A87Z97 1998
813'.52—dc21
    [B]   97-30244
                                                    CIP
                                                        AC

Printed in the United States of America

10 9 8 7 6 5 4 3 2 1

Illustration Credits: Courtesy of Willa Cather Pioneer Memorial and Educational Foundation Collection, Nebraska State Historical Society, pp. 7, 10, 14, 16, 18, 21, 26, 29, 32, 34, 39, 45, 48, 51, 57, 67, 76, 81, 85, 88, 90, 101, 106, 109.

Cover Illustration: Courtesy of Willa Cather Pioneer Memorial and Educational Foundation Collection, Nebraska State Historical Society.

Contents

A Gold Medal

On May 19, 1944, American novelist Willa Cather was presented with a gold medal. This gold medal, though, was not the kind you might expect. She did not win it for running a race with lightning speed. Nor did she win it for dancing with beauty and precision on ice skates. Willa Cather's gold medal was to honor her career as a writer. Cather's novels had charmed and sparked the imaginations of readers all over the world for almost forty years. Now she was seventy-one years old and near the end of her career. The gold medal she received was to honor the rich contributions her writing had made to American literature.

Cather's gold medal was awarded in New York City

by the National Institute of Arts and Letters. The members of this important American organization have been promoting the fine arts in America since 1898. The institute not only recognizes great American writers like Willa Cather but also honors the work of America's finest musicians, artists, sculptors, poets, and architects.

Besides the gold medal, the institute also gives several other awards. Yet the gold medal was, and still is, its highest award. Until 1951, it gave only one gold medal each year. Also, the institute rotates the medal among various fields of art. That way, the same attention and emphasis are given to different kinds of artists. So when Cather received the gold medal in 1944, it was given only once every eight years to a fiction writer.

This was not the first time Cather had been recognized for her writing. By this time in her life she had written twelve novels. In 1913, one of her first books, *O Pioneers!*, was published. The *Chicago Evening Post* called it "touched with genius."[1] Another of her books was *One of Ours*. She received the Pulitzer Prize in fiction for that book in 1923. Then in 1930 she received the Howells Medal for another novel, *Death Comes for the Archbishop*. Her picture was featured on the cover of *Time* magazine in August 1931.

Still, the institute's gold medal was different. When it was given to a writer, it was not awarded for just one book. The medal was given to honor all the works an author had produced during his or her life. Others, such as the poet Robert Frost, had been honored with the institute's gold medal in the past.

Willa Cather became one of America's finest and best-loved writers.

Poet Carl Sandburg, writer William Faulkner, and composer Leonard Bernstein would receive the gold medal in years to come. Only the best and most creative American artists could ever hope to win this high honor.

Just before the ceremony began that day in 1944, Willa Cather, small and frail, slowly rose from her chair. She made her way across the stage to greet an elderly man with white hair who was seated close by. The warmth of Willa Cather's smile showed this man's special place among her list of friends.[2] He was S. S. McClure, now eighty-seven years old. McClure was there to receive the institute's Order of Merit award. He had earned it for his work as a journalist.

With S. S. McClure there to share this special day with her, Willa Cather's life had come full circle. Almost forty years earlier, Cather's writing career began to blossom with McClure's help and encouragement. Now, on this day of honor, many years had passed. Cather was a famous American writer, with millions of loyal readers of her own. In fact, she was one of the most prominent women in America.[3]

Many of the institute members seated in the audience that day also knew Cather as a personal friend. She had loved music, literature, and art all her life. Over the years she had become friends with many of the most talented writers and artists of her time.

Many of those people also knew about Willa Cather's life. They knew that many of her experiences had shaped her writing and added to its power. Cather had begun her life in the gently rolling hills of northern Virginia. But when she was nine years old, her family moved to a distant and very different place: Nebraska. That move had a lasting impact on Cather's future.

Her adjustment to the dry, flat, unsettled Nebraska prairie was difficult. The strangeness and loneliness of that time was overwhelming.[4] Yet, it was in Nebraska that Cather made an unexpected discovery. People from faraway and strange-sounding places like Bohemia (part of what is now the Czech Republic) and Scandinavia had also come to settle in Nebraska. These people had left familiar lives behind and moved to this remote place just as Willa had. They, too, were trying to make new lives. Many were homesick and found life in Nebraska very hard. They were eager to tell their stories to anyone who would listen. Over time, young Willa Cather became one of their most eager listeners.

The friendships Willa made with these settlers helped to relieve her loneliness, too. Then, when she began to write, some of these interesting and unusual friends became models for characters in her books. From their stories also came the plots for many of her novels.

Slowly, Cather also came to respect the raw beauty and power of the Nebraska prairie. She used it as the backdrop for much of her writing. Today her name is still associated with her vivid descriptions of the Nebraska prairie and the effect it had on the people who settled there. Later she expanded the settings for her books to include other places she visited and

The Nebraska prairie was a desolate home for its early settlers. Willa Cather saw how its beauty and power shaped the lives of the people who lived there.

loved, such as the American Southwest and areas of French Canada.

This, then, was Willa Cather, one of America's finest and most important writers. She rose to receive her gold medal that day for the impact of her writing on America's literature. This talented and respected woman had indeed made her mark.

Southern Roots

Willa Cather was born on December 7, 1873. She was the first child of Mary Virginia Boak and Charles Fectigue Cather. At that time, they were living with Willa's maternal grandmother, Rachel Boak, in the Back Creek Valley of Virginia. The Back Creek Valley is in northern Virginia, near the town of Winchester. This area is known for its lush natural beauty. When she was a little girl, Willa was surrounded every day by gently rolling pastureland, meandering creeks, and wooded hills of the area.

She was named Willela Love Cather in memory of her father's younger sister. Her name also honored her mother's brother, William Lee Boak. He had been

Willa Cather was born in Virginia on December 7, 1873. She was the oldest of seven children.

killed in the Civil War, which ended just eight years before Willa was born. Like her uncle, Willa was called "Willie" by her family and friends. But while she was still a young girl, she chose to change her name to Willa. She recorded that name change herself in the Cather family Bible.

Cather's father, Charles, was a tall, handsome man with blue eyes and gentle, soft-spoken ways. Mr. Cather had studied law for two years before he married Willa's mother. He often helped the people of Back Creek Valley with their legal problems. Willa loved her father deeply and always felt close to him. She was proud that she had his fine skin and dark blue eyes.[1]

Willa's mother, Mary Virginia Boak, was known as "Jennie" to the people of Back Creek Valley. Like Charles, she had grown up there. She taught school before she married Charles in 1872. A proper, genteel southern lady, Jennie took great pride in her appearance. She often carried a parasol to match her dress and liked wearing a corsage of fresh violets.

Mrs. Cather was much more forceful than her husband. Known for her grand presence and strong personality, she ruled the family. Willa and her brothers and sisters knew that their mother expected their respect and obedience.[2] Still, even though she was strict, Mrs. Cather gave her children a lot of freedom as they were growing up. She let their individual personalities grow. She wanted her children to develop their interests and abilities as they chose.

The same year Willa Cather was born, another important event took place in the Cather family. Her

Willa Cather's mother, Mary Virginia Boak Cather, was known as "Jennie." Willa Cather inherited her mother's strong personality.

father's brother, George, moved from Virginia and took a homestead in Webster County, Nebraska. Although Willa was just a baby then, that move was to have a far-reaching impact on her life.

A homestead was a piece of raw, untouched land owned by the United States government. Beginning in 1862, Congress passed a series of homestead laws that made it possible for many people to afford farm-land in the Midwest and western parts of the United States. The government wanted the country settled with people and towns from coast to coast. Instead of paying money for a piece of land, a homesteader sim-ply had to live on a homestead for five years to become its owner.

After the Civil War ended, many people began moving west. Besides the chance to get free land from the government, people could also buy land from the railroads for very little money. The railroads, too, wanted to encourage settlement of the West. When news of these opportunities reached Europe, large numbers of foreign immigrants joined the Americans and headed west. In the 1880s, more than one million people began to fill the unsettled lands west of the Mississippi River.[3]

The land set aside by the homestead laws was often in desolate areas. Much of the land did not have enough water for farming. In many places there were not enough trees for wood to build houses or barns. In Nebraska, many homesteaders had to build their homes from sod "bricks" cut from the land.

Despite such hardships, George Cather became a successful farmer not long after settling in Nebraska

Willa Cather's father, Charles Fectigue Cather, was a soft-spoken southern gentleman. Cather always felt close to him.

in 1873. He began sending letters back home to his brother, Charles, in Virginia. In his letters he wrote of the new life he and his family were making on the prairie.

In 1877, Charles Cather's parents followed their son George to Webster County, Nebraska, and built a ranch of their own. They left their home in Virginia, called Willow Shade Farm, for Charles and his family to manage themselves.

Grandfather Cather had built the family home in the 1850s, more than twenty years before Willa was born. He named the home Willow Shade because it was surrounded by many graceful willow trees. It was a large brick home that Cather, her parents, and Grandmother Boak moved into when Willa was almost one year old.

Willow Shade was three stories tall, with five bedrooms and a two-story wing in the back. It was an ideal home for a young and growing family. Each room had a fireplace, which kept the house warm in winter. A spring from a nearby mountain gave the house a steady supply of cool water.

Willow Shade Farm was always bustling with spinning, quilting, churning, candle making, and sheep shearing. Women came from nearby to make quilts, and Willa would sometimes sit under the quilting frames and listen to the conversations of the women as they sewed. The house also provided hospitality to a steady stream of friends and relatives who came to visit the Cathers. There was always plenty of activity there to keep a growing girl busy.

Although the farm provided a few crops for the

family's use, the thin, rocky soil was too poor for much farming. Instead, Charles Cather raised sheep. Often he would carry Willa on his shoulders as he drove the sheep back into the fold in the evening. A big, four-story sheep barn was on the property, along with a mill that was used to grind feed for the sheep.

During her years in Virginia, Cather attended school in the Back Creek Valley. But mainly she learned to read and write from Grandmother Boak. Willa also came to know English literature by listening to Grandmother Boak read to her from such classics as the Bible, *The Pilgrim's Progress*, and *Peter Parley's Universal History*.

Willa also spent her days exploring the fields and woods around her home. She picked wildflowers on the hills and played in the creek that wound its way through the farm. She grew to know and love every rock and tree. Her life in Virginia was full and satisfying.[4]

But a big change was on the horizon. Cather's father became interested in the news of life in Nebraska. He began to think about joining his brother and parents and moving his family there, too. The letters they sent made Nebraska sound like a good place to live. Also, tuberculosis was a serious threat in the humid weather of the Back Creek Valley. Charles Cather knew that the hot, dry air in Nebraska would be healthier for his family. Finally, when the sheep barn burned beyond repair, Cather decided that the time had come to move west and start over.

By the time they left Virginia, Jennie and Charles Cather had added three more children to their

The Cather's large family home in Virginia was called Willow Shade. Willa Cather lived there until she was nine years old.

family—Roscoe, Douglass, and Jessica. Along with the Cather family, Grandmother Boak also got ready to move west. A nursemaid and housekeeper named Margie Anderson and her brother, Enoch, went too.

With this decision, Willa's life was turned upside down. She had to leave behind the carefree days of her life at Willow Shade. In its place, she found herself traveling into the unknown. Moving to Nebraska meant selling their beloved Willow Shade, along with most of its contents. The Cathers took only their clothes, dishes, silver, and books.

Willa also had to leave behind her favorite sheepdog, Vic. As an adult, Cather often told the story of the day she had to leave her dog. As the family boarded the train that was to take them away, Vic broke loose from her chain and came bounding toward the train hoping to join her family.[5]

It was late March 1883, and Willa was only nine years old when her family left Virginia. As the train pulled out of the small railroad depot in the Back Creek Valley to head more than a thousand miles west into the prairies of Nebraska, Willa's heart was left behind. What would the future hold?

Transplanted to Nebraska

Slowly, the Cathers made their way across the country. From the train's windows they could see new farms dotting the expanses of bare land. Homesteaders were beginning to settle more of the country. When the Cathers entered Nebraska in 1883, it had been a state for only sixteen years.

Red Cloud, in south central Nebraska, was a town of about twelve hundred people. Red Cloud had been founded just thirteen years earlier by a man named Silas Garber. The town was named for an Oglala Sioux chief who helped settle a peace treaty between the United States government and the Sioux. Red Cloud was a busy stop on the railroad, with four trains going east and four going west each day.

The Cathers ended their long journey from Virginia at Red Cloud's Republican Valley Railroad Station, which was about one mile south of town. Exhausted from their journey, the Cathers piled their belongings into several farm wagons and headed off across the prairie. They were going to Grandfather Cather's ranch, about twelve miles from Red Cloud. Willa had to steady herself against the sides of the wagon as it slowly bumped its way over the rough ground.

Peering over the wagon's sides, Willa was shocked by what she saw.[1] Unlike Virginia, with its deep, rich groves of trees and thick, green grass, Nebraska was an endless expanse of grays and browns. There were almost no trees. The stark environment influenced her thoughts and feelings so much that later she described them in one of her novels, *My Ántonia*. She wrote, "Trees were so rare in that country, and they had to make such a hard fight to grow, that we used to feel anxious about them, and visit them as if they were persons."[2]

During the ride Willa remembered fighting back tears. But her father told her that she must show grit in a new country. As she would tell an interviewer later, "I felt a good deal as if we had come to the end of everything—it was a kind of erasure of personality. . . . I would not know how much a child's life is bound up in the woods and hills and meadows around it, if I had not been jerked away from all these and thrown out into a country as bare as a piece of sheet iron."[3]

Once settled at Grandfather Cather's ranch,

Charles Cather began his life as a typical Nebraska farmer, raising corn and hogs. After a few weeks of painful homesickness for Virginia, Willa's natural curiosity began to take over. She had a lot of new territory to explore.

Nebraska's land was rough and uneven, covered with coarse prairie grasses that grew as high as six feet. Erosion laced the land with gulleys, hollows, and shallow creek beds. In spring and summer, thousands of wildflowers dotted the landscape in yellow, orange, red, and purple. Even today a visitor can walk through knee-high prairie grass, surrounded by the rustle of the wind, the songs of larks, and the chirping of insects.

When Willa moved there, she was able to see the last of the roaming buffalo, elk, and deer herds. They shared the prairie with coyotes, foxes, skunks, badgers, prairie dogs, and jackrabbits. Nebraska was also home to many different kinds of birds. Blackbirds, quail, sparrows, hawks, and owls were plentiful. Snakes also lived in the Nebraska prairie. Grandmother Cather never went to her garden without carrying the heavy, steel-tipped hickory cane that she used for killing rattlesnakes.

Riding her pony over the prairie, Willa soon began to feel better in this strange place. She also began to make friends with other families living nearby. She discovered that many of them were not Americans but had come from faraway places. The land surrounding Red Cloud was home to many people from countries such as Russia, Germany, France, and Sweden.[4]

America in the late nineteenth century had opened

Willa Cather, age ten, met many interesting people in Nebraska who later inspired characters in her books.

its unsettled land to people from all over the world. They came by the thousands, often hoping to leave behind poverty in their countries and begin new lives. Others came to escape political or religious repression. Some simply came for the promise of adventure. Nebraska was an open book waiting for new settlers to fill its pages.

The friendships Willa made suddenly began to broaden her views. Although most of the immigrants spoke little or no English, Willa was somehow able to communicate with them and to learn from them. She began to realize for the first time that the world held many interesting people and places for her to discover.[5]

To Willa, her new friendships were like chests of unexpected treasure. Each immigrant family had an interesting story to tell of life in the "old country." She loved to listen to the unusual sounds of their native languages. She found their traditions, customs, foods, and mannerisms fascinating.

In turn, the immigrants were kind to her and understood her homesickness. As she once described in an interview for the *New York Evening Post*:

> I have never found any intellectual excitement more intense than I used to feel when I spent a morning with one of these pioneer women at her baking or butter-making. I used to ride home in the most unreasonable state of excitement; I always felt as if they told me so much more than they said—as if I had got inside another person's skin.[6]

She was also impressed by the courage and determination many of these people showed by surviving in such a difficult place. When Cather began to write, the immigrants' struggles became the core of many of her stories.[7]

The homesteaders in Nebraska faced incredible problems in their struggle to cultivate this wild territory. At first, land without trees seemed to be an advantage. Without trees, the land looked ready for planting with little effort. Instead, the farmers found the hard soil, with its covering of thick prairie grass, to be very difficult to plow. Without trees, there also was no wood for building houses and barns.

Water, too, was scarce. Watering systems had to be built to get water for the crops. Many times settlers carried water by hand, sometimes for miles. The Cathers suffered from the lack of water too. They used as little as they could, trying to make any water they had last as long as possible. Sometimes it became so stale and slimy that they couldn't drink it, despite their thirst. Then they were left with the pain of swollen, cracked lips and tongues.[8]

The weather also brought hardships. The winters in Nebraska are bitter, with heavy snowfall and temperatures often below zero. In her book *My Ántonia*, Cather described snow so deep that a farmer would have to dig a tunnel through it to get from the house to the barn. In summer, the sizzling heat beats down without relief, with few trees to provide shade.

The winds that sweep across Nebraska are also well known. One account advised people to lie flat on the ground during a Nebraska windstorm to keep from blowing away.[9] Along with the heat and the fierce winds came prairie fires that could easily rage

Roscoe and Douglass were young boys when the Cathers moved to their new home on the prairie.

out of control. With the dry, hot winds of summer to drive them, fires could burn everything for miles. Tornadoes and hailstorms also plagued the settlers. As if that were not enough, thousands of grasshoppers sometimes came in great swarms to attack the crops, hungrily eating every plant in their way.

Without wood to build shelter, many Nebraska pioneers learned to make homes from the sod, or prairie soil, that covered the ground. It was held together by the thick, matted roots of the prairie grass. Houses were built fairly quickly with sod "bricks." Windows were covered with animal skins or burlap bags. In some sod houses, the ceilings were lined with cloth. In others, plaster was spread over the sod walls. Even so, it was not unusual to see a snake's head dart out from the earthen walls or from between cracks in the plaster.[10]

Another type of home on the prairie was called a dugout. This sort of home was a cave dug out of a hillside. Wooden beams were wedged at the entrance to create a door. How different from Willow Shade this new territory must have looked to young Willa Cather!

Years later, Cather described the impact her move to the Nebraska prairie had on her life:

> This country was mostly wild pasture and as naked as the back of your hand. I was little and homesick and lonely and my mother was homesick and nobody paid any attention to us. So the country and I had it out together and by the end of the first autumn, that shaggy grass country had gripped me with a passion I have never been able to shake. It has been the happiness and the curse of my life.[11]

After about eighteen months at Grandfather Cather's ranch, Charles Cather decided to move his family into the town of Red Cloud. In the short time the Cathers had been in Nebraska, the town's size had more than doubled. Thinking that the town would only continue to grow, he decided to sell farms, insurance, and loans. Once the Cathers moved into town, Red Cloud was their permanent home. As a writer, Willa Cather would use Red Cloud as the model for the towns in six of her novels.

With so many newcomers to Red Cloud, houses were scarce. Mr. Cather rented the only house available at the time. It was a light beige house at 245 Third Avenue, near the town's main street. The house quickly became crowded for the growing Cather family. During their Red Cloud years the Cathers added three more children to the family: James, Elsie, and Jack. To have enough sleeping space for everyone, the attic was made into a dormitory for the older children.

The intense heat in the attic felt like an oven in the summers. In the winters it was icy cold, with only the two house chimneys to heat it. In winter, the children took hot bricks up with them at night to help keep their feet warm in bed. They often would awaken in the morning to feel snowflakes that had drifted down through the rafters onto their cheeks.

Up the steep, narrow steps from the kitchen, the attic became Willa's sanctuary. The Cathers enclosed an area in the attic for her, and this room became her own territory. There she found the freedom and privacy to develop her imagination. To guard this privacy

With so many children, the Cather family was cramped for space
in this house in the town of Red Cloud, Nebraska.

from her brothers and sisters, Willa always locked the door whenever she left her room.

Willa's mother, Jennie, was often ill during their years in Red Cloud. Without their mother's direct supervision, the Cather children invented their own activities. One of their favorites was hurrying to the train depot whenever they heard the whistle of an approaching train, to see who was arriving. The busy railroad town brought a steady stream of new settlers. It also brought actors, who would perform in town at the newly built Red Cloud Opera House.

The children often swam and fished in the Republican River and played on a sandbar they named "Far Island." When she was older, Cather also worked at the local drugstore. Instead of money, she was paid with books and flowered wallpaper, which she used to decorate her attic room.

Willa attended school in Red Cloud, and her teachers found her to be an excellent student. From Grandmother Boak she had a broad knowledge of literature. At night in her attic room, Willa loved to read on her own. William Shakespeare, Lord Byron, Leo Tolstoy, Charles Dickens, Sir Walter Scott, Mark Twain, and Nathaniel Hawthorne were some of her favorite authors.

Like her mother, Willa had a forceful personality and very strong opinions. Many of the people she met liked her, but others found her offensive. Always an individual, Willa rebelled against the current fashions during her years in Red Cloud. She wore her hair short and often dressed boyishly. In a friend's album, she wrote that her idea of perfect misery was doing

Willa Cather found privacy in her attic bedroom. She decorated it herself with wallpaper that she earned by working at the local drugstore.

needlework; her idea of perfect happiness was "amputating limbs."[12]

Willa's interest in amputation arose from the time she spent with Dr. G. E. McKeeby. He was the Cathers' family doctor in Red Cloud. She often went with him or Dr. Damerell, another local doctor, to see patients. On one visit, Dr. Damerell let Willa give a boy an anesthetic, called chloroform, to deaden his senses before the doctor amputated his leg.

Instead of feeling disgust at such a gruesome sight, Willa decided she wanted to become a surgeon. She learned even more about surgery by dissecting dead cats, dogs, and frogs in a laboratory she set up in her father's real estate office. For a while she even signed her name as "William Cather, M.D."

Besides the town doctors, Willa found other interesting people in Red Cloud to learn from. During her piano lessons, she interrupted her German piano teacher with so many questions about his life in Germany that he had little time to teach her music. Mr. and Mrs. Weiner, who had also come to Red Cloud from Germany, introduced Willa to French literature, which she grew to love. Her favorite French author was Gustave Flaubert.

An Englishman named William Ducker was another adult who befriended Willa. He had come to Red Cloud in 1885. Although he worked as a clerk in the Red Cloud dry goods store, he was also a literature scholar, with a special fondness for Latin and Greek classics. Once Ducker's knowledge and Willa's thirst for learning came together, their relationship was set. He began teaching her Latin and Greek when she was eleven years old. Mr. Ducker also sparked Willa's interest in science. Together they often did science experiments in his garage.

Willa's sensitivity to people grew in this rich environment of varied personalities and experiences. She began to understand how the events in people's lives molded them. Cather's knowledge of people was later reflected in the characters in her books. Her realistic descriptions made her characters come alive for her readers.

Looking back on her writing, Cather later said:

The ideas for all my novels have come from things that happened around Red Cloud when I was a child. I was all over the country then, on foot, on horseback and in our farm wagons. My nose went poking into nearly everything. It happened that my mind was constructed for the particular purpose of absorbing impressions and retaining them.[13]

In 1890, Cather graduated from high school, and left Red Cloud for the first time. She moved to Lincoln, Nebraska, to begin college at the University of Nebraska. Since the entrance exams for the university were very difficult, she spent her first year of study in a college preparatory school in Lincoln. At that time she was planning to specialize in a scientific field. She was especially interested in astronomy, botany, and chemistry.

Cather began her university studies with energy and enthusiasm. Normally she got up at 5:00 A.M. to study. She often worked late into the evenings as well. As her lifelong friend Edith Lewis wrote years later, "She had always this power of intense application . . . There was nothing of it in the easygoing, drifting Southern way of her family, who loved to sit about in leisurely conversation, never hurrying to attack the day's business."[14]

Cather's study interests changed from the sciences to writing when she began her first English class. The professor, Ebenezer Hunt, became aware of Cather's talent in a paper she wrote, "The Personal Characteristics of Thomas Carlyle." Carlyle was a famous Scottish historian and essayist. Cather's essay impressed Professor Hunt so much that he sent it to a newspaper, the *Nebraska State Journal*, which published it in the spring of 1891.

The sudden attention and praise Cather received from having her paper published had a deep effect on her. The newspaper's editor and owner, Charles Gere, was also struck by Cather's talent for organizing and expressing her thoughts. He wrote that "a careful reading would convince any student of literature that it is a remarkable production, reflecting not a little credit upon the author and the university."[15] From then on, the direction of Cather's life work changed. English composition and English literature replaced the sciences as her main courses of study.

In her second year at the university, Cather began writing for her college paper, the *Hesperian*. She became the paper's managing editor and wrote editorials, articles, stories, and plays.

In 1893, Cather began writing reviews of plays for the *Nebraska State Journal*. Excellent plays often came to Lincoln and were performed at the Funke

Opera House and the Lansing Theater. Cather had been interested in the theater since her days in Red Cloud attending performances at the Red Cloud Opera House. Now, with her job writing a column called "The Passing Show," she had the chance to go to every play that came through Lincoln. She was paid one dollar for each column she wrote.

Not one to shy away from conflict, Cather readily expressed her views as a critic. Her opinions of the plays she saw were often negative. In one of her first columns, she reviewed the play *Richelieu* and its leading actor, Walker Whiteside. She wrote:

> *The main fault in his acting seems to be that he acts too much. He declaims constantly and hisses an invitation to dinner as if it were a summons to the block. . . . He pitches the key of his work too low and the key of his voice too high. . . . 'Richelieu' is a poor play; Mr. Whiteside is a poor actor, yet he can be borne; but 'Richelieu' and Whiteside together!*[16]

Many actors actually dreaded performing in Lincoln, for fear of a bad review from Willa Cather. Her readers, though, were delighted with her lively language and sharp wit.[17]

Cather graduated from the university in 1895 and returned to Red Cloud. Without a job, though, she was restless. She applied to teach at the university, but was turned down. She tried to write, but nothing she wrote pleased her.

Uncertain about her future, Cather returned to Lincoln for a visit the next year. While there, she saw the Geres, her friends who owned the *Nebraska State*

In honor of her graduation from the University of Nebraska in 1895, Willa Cather posed for this formal portrait.

Journal. They introduced her to a visitor from Pittsburgh named James Axtell. He was just starting a new magazine, the *Home Monthly*, and offered Cather a position as one of its editors. With no other job offers to consider, Cather accepted. By midsummer 1896, she had moved from Red Cloud to Pittsburgh and was ready to begin her new assignment.

Opportunity in Pittsburgh

The *Red Cloud Chief* reported Willa Cather's move to Pittsburgh in its June 26, 1896, edition. In the "City News" section, the announcement read, "Miss Willa Cather left this week for Pittsburgh, Pa., where she has a position on the *Home Magazine*. She has become one of the leading lady writers of the state, and we wish her success."[1] With that, Cather plunged into the unknown once again.

She found Pittsburgh to be a sprawling city, bustling with activity and industry. The smoky city's rivers and surrounding hills were strange sights for her after thirteen years on the Nebraska prairie. A city of four hundred thousand people, Pittsburgh was an important business center for the country. Steel was its main product. From a distance, the fires from the huge furnaces in the steel mills gave the city a reddish glow, as if the city itself were on fire.[2]

Great fortunes had been made by some of Pittsburgh's business leaders, such as Andrew Carnegie, Andrew Mellon, and George Westinghouse. The city's wealth could be seen in its many large, beautiful homes and its elegant parks and stately monuments.

Cather found that Pittsburgh was an important center for culture as well as for business. All the leading dramatic companies performed there in the late nineteenth century. The Pittsburgh Symphony had also recently been formed.

Cather was just twenty-two years old when she arrived in Pittsburgh. At first she stayed with her new employer and his wife, Mr. and Mrs. Axtell. After a few weeks, she moved into a boardinghouse at 304 South Craig Street. It was in the East End of the city, not far from the Carnegie Library.

Cather was not earning much money then, and her living conditions at the boardinghouse were rather poor. The food was terrible and her room had little furniture. Yet she saved as much money as she could to send home to help her family. During those days Cather rode a bicycle to and from the offices of the *Home Monthly*, racing the trolley cars that traveled along the streets.

The *Home Monthly* was written for women. The wives and mothers who bought the magazine were usually educated and well-to-do. Its contents included light stories and poems, recipes, and articles about raising children. To Cather, it was not the serious kind of writing that she liked or wanted to write herself.[3]

Still, Cather found her work there interesting enough to hold her for a while. Mr. Axtell also let her manage much of the magazine's production, which was a new challenge. Through her work at the *Home Monthly*, she gained helpful experience and met many interesting people.

As a new magazine, the *Home Monthly* did not have many articles ready to publish. Nor did it have the money to pay well-known writers. Cather herself wrote many of the articles and stories for the early issues. She wrote about everything from the kings and queens of Europe to the first Thanksgiving in America.[4] She signed her articles with other names so it would look as if the magazine had many writers.

She also wrote book reviews in a column called "Old Books and New." Over time, Cather critiqued many books for the column. They ranged from her old favorites to newly published works, such as Charles Dickens's *David Copperfield* and Mark Twain's *Tom Sawyer*.

While working at the *Home Monthly*, Cather met a likable German-American named George Seibel. He was a well-educated young journalist who wanted to write articles for the *Home Monthly*. Cather published some of his work, and over time their friendship grew. She found that they shared a love of French and German literature.

Once a week while she lived in Pittsburgh, Cather

visited George Seibel and his wife, Helen, in their home. After supper they spent the evening reading and translating French literature. Sometimes they baked cookies, and at Christmas Cather always helped them decorate their home. Without a family of her own in the area, the Seibels became Cather's Pittsburgh family, and she enjoyed sharing the warmth of their friendship.[5]

In addition to her work on the *Home Monthly*, Cather continued to write her weekly column, "The Passing Show," for the *Nebraska State Journal*. In this column, she reviewed Pittsburgh plays and concerts for the people in Nebraska. She often included entertaining personality sketches of the performers as well. She also began to write theater and music reviews for the Pittsburgh *Daily Leader*, the largest newspaper in Pennsylvania at that time.

Her work as drama and music critic gave Cather the chance to write about what she enjoyed. It also put her in touch with other people who shared her interest in drama, literature, art, and music. Later, as a writer, she gave many of her main characters the same deep interest in the arts that she had herself.

Just as in Nebraska, Cather's dramatic reviews ranged from wild enthusiasm to total condemnation. She expected excellence in a performance, and when she was disappointed, her opinions could be painfully brutal. Her book reviews were just as honest. She read hundreds of books each year and was no kinder to authors in her reviews than she was to actors.[6]

After a year in Pittsburgh, Cather went back to

In Pittsburgh, Willa Cather enjoyed visiting with her good friends George and Helen Seibel. Here she is writing in the library of the Seibel home.

Red Cloud to visit. While she was there, she heard that the *Home Monthly* had been sold to another company. Deciding that this was the time to cut her ties with the magazine, she resigned.

Without a job in Pittsburgh, Cather might have stayed in Red Cloud permanently. Yet she had enjoyed the culture and stimulation that Pittsburgh had to offer.[7] Luckily, in early September 1897, the Pittsburgh *Daily Leader* offered her a full-time position as drama and music critic. She eagerly accepted the job and returned to Pittsburgh.

After only a month at the *Leader*, she was promoted to the job of day telegraph editor, in addition to being the drama and music critic. As telegraph editor, she received messages about news events from reporters in foreign countries. From their messages she wrote articles for the newspaper. She usually worked from 8:00 A.M. to 2:00 P.M. at the *Leader*. On Saturdays, she worked until midnight. In the afternoons she wrote on her own, and plays or concerts occupied her evenings. Despite this hectic schedule, she also continued to write book reviews for the *Home Monthly* and theater reviews for the *Lincoln Courier* in Nebraska.

Cather also had a full life outside of work. While living in Pittsburgh, she had several suitors and at least one marriage proposal. Yet she decided she must live her life without marriage so that she could devote herself to writing. Writing and the arts were like a religion to her, she said, and required all her time and interest.[8]

It was during her time at the *Leader*, in 1899, that Cather met Isabelle McClung. Over time, McClung would become one of Cather's most important lifelong friends. McClung would also at last enable Cather to begin her career as a serious writer.

Isabelle McClung was the daughter of a well-known and respected judge in Pittsburgh. Wealthy, stern, and old-fashioned, Judge McClung lived with his wife and daughter in a large house on Murray Hill, which was one of the most elegant areas in Pittsburgh.

Isabelle McClung was known in the city for her beauty and intelligence. She also loved the arts, just as Cather did. With her family's prominence in Pittsburgh, McClung was able to meet and become friends with many writers, painters, musicians, and actors. McClung and Cather first met one evening while attending a play. By that time, Cather had become known in Pittsburgh for the reviews she wrote for the *Leader*.

McClung was delighted to meet this journalist who wrote such interesting and well-informed articles for the newspaper. Quickly, the women became friends, and McClung learned about Cather's love of literature and growing ambition to write novels.

McClung knew that Cather would have more time to write if she didn't have to worry about her food and rent and all the other time-consuming chores of daily life. So McClung persuaded Cather to move into the McClung family home. She made a study for Cather in the attic sewing room, away from the noise of the house. McClung also protected Cather's time and privacy. She turned away unwanted visitors and declined party invitations so Cather could work in peace. With

From 1900 to 1906, Cather lived in the family home of her friend Isabelle McClung in Pittsburgh. In a study set up in the attic, Cather could write without being disturbed.

McClung's help, Cather began to devote time to writing.

At the same time, Cather's work at the *Leader* was going well. Yet she knew there was something missing in her life. Despite McClung's help, Cather's job still took too much of her time and energy. In 1901, after four years at the *Leader*, Cather resigned from the newspaper to take a job as a teacher. As she said in an interview many years later:

> *I quit editorial work because it afforded me no time in which to write. The more you pursue your hobby, the more the other things drop out. The reason I didn't like my newspaper experience as telegraph editor and dramatic critic on the* Pittsburgh Daily Leader *was because it gave me so little time for the things I wanted to do.*[9]

Cather's first teaching position was at Central High School in Pittsburgh. (Later, in 1903, she changed schools and taught at Allegheny High School.) She enjoyed working with her students and she was able to teach two of her favorite subjects, English and Latin. Best of all, with her summers off, teaching was an ideal way for her to have more time to write.

One of the first things Cather taught her students was how to pronounce her name. She told them it was not pronounced "Kyther," or "Kayther," but that it rhymed with "rather." In addition, her students found her to be a strict teacher. Never settling for average work, she demanded the best her students could give. She knew that to learn to write, her students needed to write as much as possible.[10] So in addition to reading assignments, she usually had them write every day. They also had to memorize poems.

Yet her classes were never dull. Cather peppered her lectures with stories about her past and the interesting people she had known.[11] Long afterward, in 1925, Cather would give her views about education:

> *The one education which amounts to anything is learning how to do something well whether it is to make a bookcase or write a book. If I could get a carpenter to make me some good bookcases, I would have as much respect for him as I have for the people whose books I want to put on them. Making something well is the principal end of education.*[12]

In the spring of 1902, McClung and Cather took a long trip to England and France. This was Cather's first trip to Europe, and it turned out to be an unforgettable experience. She visited the places where many of her favorite authors had lived and written. In France, especially, Cather absorbed the rich culture. The peaceful countryside, the melodic language, the majestic cathedrals, and the fragrant orchards and vineyards all combined to stir her senses.

The sight of wheat fields in the French countryside reminded Cather of the Nebraska crops she knew so well. Their sight made her ache with happiness and homesickness at the same time.[13] With this trip, her imagination and creativity were broadened as never before. The time she spent in these new places gave her a deeper sensitivity to life, which she would draw upon later in writing her stories. Throughout her life,

In 1903, Willa Cather was working as a teacher in Pittsburgh. Being a teacher instead of a newpaper editor gave her more time to work on her writing, especially during summer recess.

Cather's fascination with Europe would pull her back there time and time again to visit and to explore.

Once she was back in Pittsburgh, Cather's writing continued to improve. By this time, well-known magazines such as the *Ladies' Home Journal* and the *Saturday Evening Post* were buying her stories and poems regularly. Then, in 1903, Cather's first book, *April Twilights*, was published. It contained thirty-seven of her poems.

Cather wrote about the things that were important to her. Her poems were about family, love and loss, friends, and nature. Her most famous poem is "Grandmother, Think Not I Forget." It is about a woman who mourns her grandmother's death and remembers the love and support her grandmother will no longer be able to give her. Cather wrote it in memory of her Grandmother Boak, who had died while Cather was in college.

Although *April Twilights* did not sell very well, it was an important step in Cather's career. It gave her a wider audience of readers than ever before. She also was noticed and reviewed by literary critics for the first time. Generally, they were very positive about the book. *The New York Times* said Cather showed promise as a poet.[14] The *Chicago Tribune* called *April Twilights* the "work of a real poet."[15]

At last, Cather's writing career was beginning in earnest. When *April Twilights* was published, Cather was not even thirty years old. She had no idea of all that still lay ahead.

The Spell of
S. S. McClure

In addition to the publication of *April Twilights*, 1903 brought another momentous change in Cather's life that propelled her writing career forward. Early that year, Cather's work came to the attention of a man named S. S. McClure.

Samuel S. McClure, or "S. S.," as he was called, was an important and well-known magazine publisher. Charming and energetic, he published *McClure's*, one of the most respected and successful magazines of its day. *McClure's* was known especially for its fine stories. Robert Louis Stevenson, Arthur Conan Doyle, Thomas Hardy, Mark Twain, and Walt Whitman had all written for *McClure's*. S. S. McClure was always scouting for talented new writers for the magazine.

As events unfolded, McClure's cousin was traveling through Lincoln, Nebraska, seeking undiscovered writing talent. While there, he met with Cather's former boss from the *Nebraska State Journal*, who recommended Willa Cather as a gifted new writer. After receiving this enthusiastic tip, McClure himself wrote to Cather in late March, requesting samples of her work.

McClure didn't know that Cather had already submitted some of her stories to the magazine. They had been returned to her as not up to the magazine's standards. So with low expectations, Cather again sent some of her work to S. S. McClure for his personal review.

What happened next would change Cather's life. McClure was so impressed with her stories that he immediately sent her a telegram. He told her that he was very interested in her work and that he wanted to see her in his New York office as soon as possible. McClure saw Cather as a rising new talent in the writing world.[1]

On May 1, 1903, Cather met with S. S. McClure. In his typical way, he overwhelmed her with enthusiasm about her work. He wanted to know everything about her and began making plans to publish her stories. By the time she left New York, Willa Cather knew that her writing was finally getting the attention it needed. McClure had made her feel important. She was exuberant and hopeful about the future.[2]

Word of Cather's promising interview with McClure spread to her friends in Nebraska. The *Nebraska State Journal* wrote:

> *Miss Willa Cather of Pittsburgh, who is so well
> known to the Nebraska readers of the Journal and
> to the people of Lincoln, was in the city this week.
> She was summoned by the McClure people who have
> of late taken a lively interest in her literary work. It
> is said that an arrangement has been made for the
> publication of some of her stories in the magazine. To
> be taken up by Mr. McClure is counted a decided
> recognition, and Miss Cather's friends will under-
> stand that this means that she has "arrived."* [3]

One of the stories Cather had sent to McClure was
called "A Wagner Matinee." It is about a woman who
gave up her talent as a pianist for a rugged life as a
Nebraska pioneer wife. When she visits the city of
Boston, she is painfully reminded of all the talent and
beauty she has lost forever. In the story, Cather
describes life in the West very much as it was during
her childhood days in Red Cloud, without culture or
beauty. In contrast, Boston is portrayed as a glitter-
ing center of music, art, and culture.

Along with "A Wagner Matinee," Cather sent
McClure another story, "The Sculptor's Funeral." It is
about a sculptor who lives in a small town where the
people think art is a waste of time. Finally he moves
to a big city in the East. With education and encouragement to help his talent grow, he becomes a
world-famous artist.

In February 1904, "A Wagner Matinee" was
published in another magazine, *Everybody's Magazine.*
Despite S. S. McClure's enthusiasm, many people in
Nebraska were insulted by Cather's harsh description

of the West. As one reviewer wrote in the *Nebraska State Journal*:

> *The stranger to this state will associate Nebraska with the aunt's wretched figure, her ill-fitting false teeth, her skin yellowed by weather. . . . If the writers of fiction who use western Nebraska as material would look up now and then and not keep their eyes and noses in the cattle yards, they might be more agreeable company.*[4]

In her defense, Cather said that she meant her description as a tribute to the pioneers who settled the primitive Western territories.[5]

McClure's published "The Sculptor's Funeral," along with another story, "Paul's Case," in 1905. "Paul's Case" has become one of Cather's most well-known stories. It is about a high school student in Pittsburgh who is bored with his life and longs for more excitement. He runs away to New York and lives extravagantly, finding at least for a while the excitement he wanted. Finally, though, his father comes to take him back home. Rather than return, Paul chooses to end his life by quietly stepping in front of an oncoming train. Cather's theme in this story concerns the endurance a person needs to rise above the drabness of the real world, which can so easily destroy creativity and beauty.

In 1905, McClure published Cather's collection of stories in a book called *The Troll Garden*. Beautifully bound, with elegant gold lettering on the cover, *The Troll Garden* was Cather's first book of prose. All the stories are about art and artists. The

Cather (right) and Isabelle McClung shared many interests. This photograph was taken during a camping trip in Wyoming.

title for the book was taken from a work by Charles Kingsley, *The Roman and the Teuton*. In it, Kingsley writes: "A fairy palace, with a fairy garden; . . . Inside the trolls dwell, . . . working at their magic forges, making and making always things rare and strange."[6] Cather considers the artists' talents in her stories to be "rare and strange" and easily destroyed.[7]

To Cather's disappointment, reviews for *The Troll Garden* were not very positive. Many critics didn't like the odd characters and the negative, uncomfortable tone of many of the stories. In one magazine, the *Bookman*, a reviewer referred to them as "freak stories that are either lurid, hysterical or unwholesome."[8] Looking back on her reaction to the reviews, Cather later said:

> *An author is seldom sensitive except about his first volume. Any criticism of that hurts. Not criticism of its style—that only spurs one on to improve it. But the root-and-branch kind of attack is hard to forget. Nearly all very young authors write sad stories in revolt against everything. Humor, kindliness, tolerance come late.*[9]

In March 1906, a year after *The Troll Garden* was published, McClure decided he wanted Cather to move to New York and join his staff. He went to visit her in Pittsburgh to persuade her to accept his offer. Elizabeth Moorhead, a friend of Cather's in Pittsburgh, described the trip:

> *It was an exciting event indeed when S. S. McClure, who had been a mere name, a sort of far-off benignant deity, descended in the flesh upon*

Pittsburgh. . . . Once, landing in New York, he had
gone straight from the boat to his office, had found a
bundle of manuscript on his desk tied up to be
returned, and opened and read—and here he was in
Pittsburgh to see the author in person.[10]

McClure's offer presented Cather with a big
decision. The opportunity to work for the famous
magazine was tempting. Yet she had lived in
Pittsburgh for ten years and was comfortable there.
She had made many friends, enjoyed her teaching,
and had built a life that was satisfying.[11]

Cather also thought teaching was a more secure
job than working for a magazine. She was very aware
of the importance of having a steady income. She
remembered seeing her family and many of her
friends struggle during hard times when the crops
failed in Nebraska. Working at *McClure's* offered her
more excitement and money than teaching did. Still,
how secure would it be?

After three months, she decided to make the move
to New York. In a farewell letter to her students, she
expressed her regret at leaving teaching: "So I turn to
a work I love with very real regret that I must leave
behind, for the time at least, a work I had come to love
almost as well."[12]

Cather moved from Pittsburgh to New York in the
summer of 1906. She was hired at a time when it was
unusual for a woman to have a professional job.
Publishing was definitely considered a man's world.
Still, she started as an associate editor just when
most of *McClure's* staff had resigned to start a new
publication, *The American Magazine*.

McClure's offices were on East Twenty-third Street in what was then the heart of the city's publishing district. It was the kind of workplace you might expect of a busy and popular magazine. The offices were not fancy, and they were filled with the rapid metallic clicking of typewriters churning out articles. Reporters and editors dashed about as they rushed to meet their deadlines.

With so much hustle and bustle, working at *McClure's* was like working in a hurricane. Of course, everything revolved around S. S. McClure.[13] His energetic and creative personality kept the whole office in a flurry. McClure wore white sneakers to work and kept a bottle of milk on his desk to ease the ulcers he had developed from the stress.

When she came to work at *McClure's*, Cather was thirty-two years old. Her job as an editor was to buy fiction and poetry for the magazine. At five feet three inches tall, she was short and rather stocky, with clear blue eyes and reddish-brown hair that she parted in the middle. Her informal, open style and warm smile were very different from S. S. McClure's domineering personality. Yet Cather was not frightened by McClure's forceful energy. Throughout their years of working together they always shared a respect for each other and for good writing.

When she moved to New York, Cather found a small apartment in Greenwich Village, just off Washington Square. At that time, Washington Square was one of the most charming places in New York City. On the north side was a row of stately red-brick homes owned by some of New York's most well-to-do families. On the south side were simple apartments and studios where struggling artists, writers, and musicians lived.

The atmosphere in Greenwich Village was friendly and informal. Little shops and restaurants dotted the neighborhood. There was an air of youthfulness and optimism for the future. Carriages mingled with new-fangled automobiles on the streets, just as creativity and tradition lived side by side in this easygoing neighborhood.

Still with very little money, Cather lived in a house that had been divided into several apartments. She shared a bathroom at the end of the hall with other tenants. A friend, Edith Lewis, also lived in the same building.

Cather and Lewis had met years earlier in Lincoln, Nebraska. At the time, Lewis had just graduated from Smith College in Massachusetts and was back in Lincoln for the summer. Also wanting to be a writer, Lewis had published several articles in the *Lincoln Courier* and was a fan of Cather's column, "The Passing Show," in the *Nebraska State Journal*.

Now that they lived in the same building so far from their roots, the friendship between Cather and Lewis continued to grow. At Cather's suggestion, *McClure's* hired Lewis as a proofreader, and she worked with Cather on some of her assignments. Later, Lewis went on to become a magazine editor, and then an advertising writer.

The two women had many things in common. Besides writing, they were both from Nebraska, were well educated, and had similar interests and tastes in the arts. Both enjoyed travel and had simple lifestyles.

New York had even more of the arts and culture to offer Cather than Pittsburgh had. The city provided all she could take in, and more. One of her greatest pleasures was attending performances at the Metropolitan Opera, which she later did as often as twice a week. She also enjoyed the rich exotic food she found in her favorite New York restaurants. According to Cather, the Waldorf hotel "was the place to go and eat oysters at midnight."[14] She also enjoyed Delmonico's Restaurant and wrote of its tables "heavily draped in damask, with napkins as big as door-mats."[15]

After eight months at *McClure's*, Cather got her first big assignment. McClure wanted her to work on a biography of a controversial woman named Mary Baker Eddy, who lived in Boston. Cather packed her bags once again to begin the next chapter of her life.

Boston Artists

In 1906, when Cather first came to work for *McClure's*, the magazine had begun to print articles about social concerns, as well as the fiction for which it was known. The articles exposed some of the problems of society, such as dishonesty in the police forces, corrupt politicians, and unsafe working conditions.

People at that time were also very interested in knowing more about Mary Baker Eddy. Thirty years before, Mrs. Eddy had begun a religious movement called the Church of Christ, Scientist. Cather's first major assignment at *McClure's* was to learn the details about Mrs. Eddy and this new religion. To research her story, Cather would have to spend a lot of time in Boston, where Mrs. Eddy had started her church.

McClure chose Cather for this job because, according to her friend Elizabeth Sergeant, she "inspired confidence, had the mind of a judge, and the nose of a detective when she needed it."[1] The story took Cather eighteen months to finish. It became a series of articles that ran in *McClure's* in fourteen installments.

McClure was delighted with Cather's work on the Eddy story. Once it was published, it received many good reviews, and the magazine's readership grew. Cather's time in Boston was also important because of some of the people she met there.

Two of the first people Cather met in Boston were the notable lawyer Louis Brandeis and his wife, Alice. Mr. Brandeis was later appointed to the U.S. Supreme Court. Realizing Cather's interest in literature, Alice Brandeis introduced her to Mrs. Annie Fields in February 1908.

Mrs. Fields was the widow of James T. Fields of the Ticknor and Fields publishing firm. Under Mr. Fields's leadership, Ticknor and Fields had led the way in promoting American authors. Mr. Fields had published nearly all the greatest English and American writers of his day. He had also become friends with most of the writers he worked with.

The Fields's home in Boston was a gathering place for many of these authors. Mr. and Mrs. Fields often would be joined for breakfast on Sunday mornings by the greatest writers of that time.[2] The English author Charles Dickens often stayed in their old brick home during his lecture tours in America. Other famous authors, including Nathaniel Hawthorne, Ralph Waldo Emerson, James Russell Lowell, Oliver Wendell Holmes, and Henry Wadsworth Longfellow, had been guests there as well. Cather later wrote:

> *For a period of sixty years, Mrs. Fields' Boston house, at 148 Charles Street, extended its hospitality to the aristocracy of letters and art. During that long stretch of time there was scarcely an American of distinction in art or public life who was not a guest in that house; scarcely a visiting foreigner of renown who did not pay his tribute there.*[3]

By visiting with Mrs. Fields, Cather entered this rare environment of intelligence, culture, and creativity. Its peaceful air of civility made the home seem "absolutely safe from everything ugly" to Cather.[4] As she later marveled to Elizabeth Sergeant: "Think . . . what it is to know someone who invited to her table Emerson, Holmes, Hawthorne, Howells, James Russell Lowell—and who remembers and quotes what they said there!"[5]

Of the many people Cather met in the Fields's home, one who became especially important in her life was Sarah Orne Jewett. Almost sixty years old when Cather met her, Miss Jewett was a well-known author who lived part of each year with Mrs. Fields. Her most famous stories were about life in New England. Cather had long admired Jewett's work and now had the chance to become friends with her.

In her book *Not Under Forty*, Cather describes Jewett on the day they met as "very like the youthful picture of herself in the game of 'Authors,'" which she had played as a girl.[6]

Cather portrayed Jewett as "a lady, in the old high sense. It was in her face and figure, in her carriage, her smile, her voice, her way of greeting one. There was an ease, a graciousness, a light touch in conversation, a delicate unobtrusive wit."[7]

Jewett's health was very weak when she and Cather met. Their friendship lasted only sixteen months, until Jewett's death. But during that time they enjoyed many visits and often wrote letters to each other.

Jewett seemed to sense from the beginning of their friendship that Cather had important writing ahead of her. Aside from encouragement and guidance, she influenced Cather in several ways. She was concerned that Cather was trying to write while also working full time. She thought Cather could never fully develop her talent if her time and energy were always first directed at *McClure's*. In one letter to Cather, Jewett wrote, " . . . if you don't keep and guard and mature your force and above all, have time and quiet to perfect your work, you will be writing things not much better than you did five years ago."[8] These words stayed with Cather over the next few years as she continued her struggle to balance work and writing.

Jewett also influenced Cather in another way. She encouraged her to reach into the depths of her soul and revive her love of Nebraska, rather than to continue writing bitterly about the West as she had in "The Sculptor's Funeral" and "A Wagner Matinee." At

In this 1912 portrait, Willa Cather is wearing a necklace given to her by her friend and mentor, Sarah Orne Jewett. The well-known author was an important influence on Cather.

first this advice did not change Cather's approach. In time, though, it would lead her to write some of her most important and far-reaching work.

In Boston, Cather also met Ferris Greenslet, an editor for the Houghton Mifflin publishing company. Like S. S. McClure, Greenslet recognized Cather's talents of expressiveness and sensitivity. He later became the editor of her first four novels.

In 1908, Cather returned to her apartment in Washington Square. Despite her success with the Eddy story, Sarah Orne Jewett's earlier words of warning began to ring true. Edith Lewis wrote that the years just after Cather's return to New York were years of uncertainty.[9] She couldn't decide what to do. If she left *McClure's*, would she be able to support herself by writing alone? If she stayed at the magazine, how would she ever be able to write as she longed to? Willa Cather's frustration continued to build.

In 1911, Cather began work on her first novel, which she called "Alexander's Bridge." The story was based on an actual event in 1907 in which a bridge in Quebec collapsed while it was being built. The chief engineer and many of the construction workers were killed.

In the fall of 1911 Cather got permission for an extended leave of absence from *McClure's* so she could write. With Isabelle McClung, her friend from Pittsburgh, Cather rented an old house in Cherry Valley, New York. McClung thought this area, where her mother had grown up, would be perfect for Cather.

At Cherry Valley, Cather now worked on her book for hours each day. With McClung to protect her privacy, she finally found the quiet that she needed. After periods of great concentration, she would take short breaks to hike in the countryside, rain or shine. In letters she wrote to S. S. McClure about her leave of absence, she told him that she needed exactly this kind of life and had not felt so well or been so happy for several years.[10] At Cherry Valley, Cather was able to finish her book.

The story is about a world-famous bridge engineer named Bartley Alexander. He grew up in the West but later moved to Boston. The book ends with the construction of Alexander's best work, a bridge over the St. Lawrence River. Engineering flaws cause the bridge to collapse, and Alexander himself is killed in the disaster. Cather links the weaknesses that caused the bridge's collapse to the flaws in Alexander's own personality. In the end he was destroyed by both.

With the title "Alexander's Masquerade," *McClure's* published this work in installments, beginning in February 1912. That same year Houghton Mifflin published it as a novel, titled *Alexander's Bridge*. Although not reviewed widely, the book was favorably received. Most critics saw promise in Cather's work.[11] Yet soon after it was published, Cather looked back upon it critically, calling it "shallow" and "superficial."[12]

After finishing *Alexander's Bridge*, Cather began a story called "The Bohemian Girl." This story was quite different from anything she had ever written. It was about Nebraska. The Swedish and Bohemian immigrants she had known while growing up in Red Cloud were its main characters. With this story she took Sarah Orne Jewett's advice from years before to write about what she knew and loved—Nebraska. Finally Willa Cather was writing a story from her heart. Of her work up to that time, she said, "I had been trying to sing a song that did not lie in my voice."[13]

About her work on "The Bohemian Girl," Cather wrote:

> *I found it a much more absorbing occupation than writing* Alexander's Bridge; *a different process altogether. Here there was no arranging or 'inventing'; everything was spontaneous and took its own place, right or wrong. This was like taking a ride through a familiar country on a horse that knew the way, on a fine morning, when you felt like riding. The other was like riding in a park, with someone not altogether congenial, to whom you had to be talking all the time.*[14]

This tale was not just a change of direction for Cather. It was completely different from the kind of fiction that was popular with the public then. By the early 1900s the Victorian era had just ended. People were still buying romance and adventure books by authors like Rudyard Kipling and Robert Louis Stevenson. The characters they were used to reading about were upper-class people from exciting places. No one was writing about dreary farmers and working people from small towns in remote places like Nebraska. As Cather herself put it, "Since I wrote this book for myself, I ignored all the situations and accents that were then generally thought to be necessary. The 'novel of the soil' had not then come into fashion in this country."[15] Because of that, Cather didn't think the public would like "The Bohemian Girl."

McClure's was eager to see what Cather had written on her leave of absence. Nervously, she gave it to them to read. To her astonishment, *McClure's* wanted to publish the story and offered her a high price for it—$750. "The Bohemian Girl" appeared in the magazine in August 1912.

"The Bohemian Girl" was even more popular with the magazine's readers than "Alexander's Masquerade." Cather was puzzled and delighted at the same time. All her ideas about what readers wanted were turned upside down.[16] She was amazed that people enjoyed reading about immigrants, and that they would be interested in pioneer life in Nebraska. As her friend Edith Lewis wrote later, "Except for some of the people who lived in it, I think no one had ever found Nebraska beautiful until Willa Cather wrote about it."[17]

In the meantime, *McClure's* was undergoing a drastic change in management. Throughout her time at *McClure's*, Cather and S. S. had maintained their relationship of mutual admiration, trust, and loyalty. When S. S. McClure retired as editor-in-chief, Cather was extremely upset.

Years later, in one of her many interviews, Cather spoke of what she learned while at *McClure's*:

> *The six years I spent on 'McClure's Magazine' in an editorial capacity, I call work. It was during the six*

years . . . that I came to have a definite idea about writing. In reading manuscripts submitted to me, I found that 95 percent of them were written for the sake of the writer—never for the sake of the material. The writer wanted to express his clever ideas, his wit, his observations.

Almost never, did I find a manuscript that was written because a writer loved his subject so much he had to write about it.

Usually when I did get such a manuscript it was so crude it was ineffective. Then I realized that one must have two things—strong enough to mate together without either killing the other—else one had better change his job. I learned that a man must have a technique and a birthright to write—I do not know how else to express it. He must know his subject with an understanding that passes understanding. . . . [18]

Cather's years with the magazine had been good ones. She gained many valuable experiences, met many interesting people, and traveled widely. Her work had brought her more confidence and knowledge about writing than ever before.

Yet the job had become too demanding to leave her with much energy or imagination. With McClure no longer there to work with her, Cather resigned from *McClure's* in 1912. Her path was now clear to pursue her dream.

The Allure
of the West

With two books behind her, Cather had a new sense of success. Looking for a change of pace and scenery, she set off for the southwestern United States in April 1912. She wanted to visit her brother Douglass. He worked for the Santa Fe Railroad and lived in a small bungalow in Winslow, Arizona. Willa and Douglass had always been close, and they had long talked of exploring the Southwest together. She had traveled as far as Colorado before, but this was the farthest west Cather had ever gone. This trip would change the direction of much of her future work.

Cather found Winslow itself to be barren and depressing. To her, the town was dull and unappealing, with cheap, ugly shacks and tin cans whirling through the streets.[1] The dry Arizona wind only added to Winslow's sense of loneliness.

After two weeks in Winslow, though, she began to travel into the surrounding countryside. Nearby she discovered a little Mexican village that she found delightful.[2] As she continued exploring, her enchantment with the beauty of the Southwest began to grow. She warmed to the charm and culture of the people who had settled there. In Edith Lewis's words, "A whole new landscape—not only a physical landscape, but a landscape of the mind, peopled with wonderful imaginings opened out before her."[3]

Cather soon became well acquainted with the Mexicans and American Indians in the area. A Catholic priest, Father Connolly, let her go with him as he made his rounds to the tiny American Indian and Mexican churches he served. He also began teaching her Spanish. Just as in Nebraska, Cather began to sense the attachment these people had to the land they had struggled to tame. She saw again how those battles had shaped their lives.

She and Douglass next spent time camping in the hills around Winslow. Every morning for several days they loaded a wagon with canteens, coffee, fruit, and other gear, and set off. Exploring this rugged territory, Cather put her experience riding, hiking, and camping to good use. It was as if she were a tomboy again, just as in her Red Cloud days, investigating along the Republican River.[4]

Next, Cather ventured into New Mexico. There she spent time in the city of Albuquerque. To her delight, it was surrounded by American Indian villages and the ghost towns of Spanish missions that had been there since the time of the Spanish explorers. Cather especially loved the color, history, and music she found there.

Then Cather visited the Grand Canyon, where she rode a mule down into the canyon itself. It would be seven years before the Grand Canyon would become a national park, and the area was completely unspoiled by shops and tourist attractions.

After that, she and Douglass visited the cliff dwellings in Walnut Canyon, near Flagstaff, Arizona. Cliff dwellings are the remains of ancient homes that were built hundreds of years ago. Some cliff dwellings were carved directly into the porous cliff rock. These ancient homes were often several stories high, and contained rooms for sleeping, eating, and worshiping. Together, they combined to make complete towns.

There are many ruins of cliff dwellings in canyons and mesas throughout the Southwest. The nearly three hundred dwellings at Walnut Canyon are especially well preserved and date back about one thousand years.

Cather was deeply moved by all she saw at Walnut Canyon and found the dwellings hauntingly beautiful. To her, they were a symbol of human beings' attempt to endure and to create beauty in the world.[5]

Many of the things Cather saw and the people she met on that first trip to the Southwest were fixed forever in her mind. When she returned home from her western adventures, the territory kept its hold on her spirit.

Cather and her brother Douglass visited the ancient American Indian cliff dwellings at Walnut Canyon in Arizona. She later wrote about these mysterious ruins in several of her novels.

Cather's next book began as two stories. She had written one, "Alexandra," in Cherry Valley in 1911, while on leave of absence from *McClure's*. She wrote the other, "The White Mulberry Tree," when she returned from her first trip out West. Over time she combined the two into what would become one of her best-loved novels, *O Pioneers!* It was named for the poem "Pioneer! O Pioneer!" by Walt Whitman.

The story is about a pioneer family in Nebraska as they struggle to make a life for themselves in a very difficult land. As Cather said later in an interview:

> *I knew every farm, every tree, every field in the region around my home and they all called out to me. My deepest feelings were rooted in this country because one's strongest emotions and one's most vivid mental pictures are acquired before one is fifteen. I had searched for books telling about the beauty of the country I loved, its romance, the heroism and strength and courage of its people that had been plowed into the very furrows of its soil and I did not find them. And so I wrote* O Pioneers![6]

In the book's main character, Alexandra Bergson, Cather created a character who had the strength, dignity, and simplicity of the Nebraska prairie.[7] In *O Pioneers!*, as well as in another novel she would write, *My Ántonia*, the main characters are immigrants from Europe. They are molded into Americans by the prairie's power. As a girl, Willa Cather had seen this effect that the prairie had on immigrants. The themes of these two books honor the dignity of facing hardship.

As with "The Bohemian Girl," Cather wasn't sure

if the public would like this story. It was an unusual kind of book for its day. It had no clear plot or exciting action. This was a story of people's lives on the prairie. Still, with this book Cather had done exactly what she had wanted; this was the story she had always wanted to write.[8]

Writing of her concerns about *O Pioneers!*, Cather said, "I did not in the least expect that other people would see anything in a slow-moving story, without 'action,' without 'humor,' without a 'hero'; a story concerned entirely with heavy farming people, with cornfields and pasture lands and pig yards—set in Nebraska, of all places!"[9]

To Cather's relief, her old friend and editor Ferris Greenslet was enthusiastic about the book. Houghton Mifflin published it in 1913. Cather dedicated the book to her friend Sarah Orne Jewett, who had encouraged her to write about her homeland.

O Pioneers! proved Cather's genius as a writer. With it, she created an original and fresh type of story, establishing herself as an author of unusual creativity. The public responded with enthusiasm, and *O Pioneers!* became a classic in American literature.

The book's publication marked a definite change in Cather's career. Widely reviewed, *O Pioneers!* was almost universally praised. *The New York Times* critic said it was American "in the best sense of the word."[10] The *Chicago Evening Post* called it "touched with genius." Although Cather still wasn't earning very much money from her books, she now felt sure of the direction her life should take.[11]

In the fall of 1912, Cather and Edith Lewis moved

into a new apartment. Also in Washington Square, it was much more comfortable than their first apartment had been. They would live there for fifteen years.

The building at 5 Bank Street was a wide, five-story brick home. It had been built by a brewer as a wedding present for his son. Later it was made into apartments. With a broad staircase in the middle of the house, it was divided into two apartments on each floor.

Cather and Lewis rented one of the apartments on the second floor. It had seven large rooms, with high ceilings and big windows. It was just the sort of airy, spacious place that Cather wanted. They used the three front rooms as one large living room. It later became a frequent gathering place for their friends. The living room fireplace had a white marble mantel and a coal grate. The women carried their own coal up the stairs to make fires.

The building had very thick walls, which kept the apartment comfortable and quiet. A German family lived in the apartment above, and Cather could faintly hear the daughter practicing the piano in the mornings. Rather than annoy Cather, this became a kind of signal that it was time to begin her work for the day.

Cather's years at 5 Bank Street were her best writing years. She and Lewis hired a French woman, Josephine Bourda, to be their housekeeper and cook. Josephine spoke no English, so they communicated with her as best they could in broken French. She was a valuable addition to their household, adding energy, optimism, and humor. Over the years,

Josephine Bourda helped Cather and Lewis give many formal dinner parties in their apartment. They often entertained actors, artists, and writers.

With little money, Cather and Lewis furnished the apartment with secondhand items they bought at auctions. They saved any extra money for the things they found important: fresh flowers, entertaining their friends, and tickets to the theater and opera.

Opera was flourishing in New York, and *McClure's* asked Cather to write an article about it for the magazine. As part of her research, she interviewed one of opera's rising stars, Olive Fremstad. Born in Sweden, the mezzo-soprano had grown up in Minnesota. Her singing brought life to many of the great roles written by composer Richard Wagner. That first interview led to a lasting friendship between the two women. They often visited each other, sharing dinner or tea.

Fremstad became the inspiration for Cather's next novel, *The Song of the Lark*. It is about a woman named Thea Kronberg, who is gifted with a magnificent voice. Thea is driven to develop her talent despite discouragement at home. A lot of Cather herself was written into the book, for Thea realizes as a girl that she is different from other children because of her talent. Thea, like Cather, chooses a different road in life by deciding not to marry and have children. Instead, she devotes her life to her talent. In the book, Thea Kronberg also visits the cliff dwellings of the Southwest and experiences them as an important event in her life, just as Cather did.

Cather completed *The Song of the Lark* early in

A view of the living room of Cather's home in Red Cloud and her parents' bedroom. Cather described her childhood home in The Song of the Lark.

1915 and sent it to Ferris Greenslet. Although he was pleased with it, Greenslet suggested a number of changes. He thought the book was too long and detailed. Her English publisher, William Heinemann, turned it down for the same reason. He thought she had "taken the wrong road" and that the "full-blooded method, which told everything about everybody," was not her best style.[12]

After some changes, *The Song of the Lark* was published in October 1915. The book received many positive reviews, although it did not sell as many copies as Cather had hoped. She was pleased, though, that her friend Olive Fremstad was delighted with it.

8

A Single Purpose

In the summer of 1915, Cather returned to the Southwest. This time she was joined by her friend Edith Lewis. They rode the train from Chicago, traveling all day through the familiar prairies of Nebraska toward their destination: Mesa Verde in southwestern Colorado.

Mesa Verde means "green table" in Spanish. It was named for the thick green forests of juniper and piñon trees that cover its flat top. The mesa rises sharply for two thousand feet from the valleys of the Mancos and Montezuma rivers. At its highest point, it towers eighty-five hundred feet above sea level. Thousands of years of erosion have cut many deep canyons into the face of the rock.

Mesa Verde contains the best-known cliff dwellings in the United States. Although several of the dwellings were explored in 1874, the main sections were discovered in 1888, just twenty-seven years before Cather's trip there.

A rancher named Dick Wetherill discovered the dwellings by accident. He was crossing the Mancos River on his horse, searching for some lost cattle. To his surprise, he stumbled upon the entire city of cliff houses, which had been hidden for centuries.

Today Mesa Verde is a popular tourist attraction. When Cather and Lewis were there, however, it was still a very remote area. It had been open to visitors for only a few years. No cars could travel to Mesa Verde then. The women had to hire a team of horses and a driver to take them the last twenty miles. They camped in a tent in the national park that had been created in 1906 to preserve the area.

Cather and Lewis spent a week exploring Mesa Verde. The terrain was very rugged and often dangerous, but the women did not hesitate to follow their interests. They fearlessly scaled rocky cliffs and descended into steep canyons. As Edith Lewis described later, " . . . in climbing down to the bottom of Soda Canyon, we had in many places to hang from a tree or rock and then drop several feet to the next rock."[1]

The most famous dwelling at Mesa Verde is called the Cliff Palace. It contains more than two hundred rooms and twenty-three ceremonial chambers. Cather and Lewis spent one entire day just exploring the Cliff Palace. Ten years later, Cather would

Willa Cather enjoys a picnic at the Red Cloud golf course.

describe it in a novel, *The Professor's House*: "I knew at once . . . that I had come upon the city of some extinct civilization, hidden away in this inaccessible mesa for centuries, preserved in the dry air and almost perpetual sunlight like a fly in amber, guarded by the cliffs and the river and the desert."[2]

After leaving Mesa Verde, Cather and Lewis spent a week in Taos, New Mexico, located in the foothills of the Sangre de Cristo Mountains in north central New Mexico. Taos has been a gathering place for artists since the end of the nineteenth century. Cather was drawn there by the Pueblo village of San Geronimo de Taos. It is an ancient American Indian village with multistoried adobe homes that lies just north of Taos. American Indians have lived there for at least eight hundred years.

Cather and Lewis took long horseback rides to explore the surrounding territory and the Mexican villages that had sprung up there. They rode around the hilly countryside just as Cather had ridden on the prairie as a girl to visit her European neighbors.[3]

Several years later, Cather spoke to an interviewer about her trips to the Southwest:

> People will tell you that I come west to get ideas for a new novel or material for a new novel, as though a novel could be conceived by running around with a pencil and jotting down phrases and suggestions. I don't even come west for local color. I could not say, however, that I don't come west for inspiration. I do get freshened up by coming out here.[4]

Throughout her visits to the Southwest, Cather

never took notes or kept a diary to record what she saw or felt. Everything was locked in her mind, expanding her imagination. Now she had new material to think about, to draw from, and from which she would create some of her finest work.

In 1917, Cather began to work on her next book, *My Ántonia*. For three months she worked hard, and by the end of March she was halfway through the first draft.

A year earlier, her longtime friend from Pittsburgh, Isabelle McClung, had married violinist Jan Hambourg. In the late summer of 1917, the Hambourgs invited Cather to join them for a visit at the Shattuck Inn in Jaffrey, New Hampshire. This was Cather's first lengthy stay in New England, and she was enchanted.

At the Shattuck Inn, Cather lived in two small rooms on the top floor. There she continued work on *My Ántonia*. It was very much like writing in her old attic room in Red Cloud when she was a girl. Through the windows she could see the surrounding woods and pastureland, with Mount Monadnock in the distance.

The owners of the inn made sure that Cather's privacy was protected while she stayed there. The inn's bellboy, who lived in the room next to hers, was also told to be very quiet so Cather could work in peace.

Two other friends of Cather's had rented a home in Jaffrey, called "High Mowing." They set up a small tent for her in their meadow so Cather could work there, too. She would walk the half mile or so from the inn along an old road and through the woods, arriving at her outpost to work for two to three hours in the

One of Cather's favorite places to write was the Shattuck Inn in Jaffrey, New Hampshire, where she could escape from the noise of everyday life.

mornings. The remoteness and beauty there gave her another ideal setting for writing. In the afternoons Cather took long walks and explored Mount Monadnock.

From then on, the Shattuck Inn was one of her favorite places to write. Over the next years she spent many autumns in Jaffrey after the summer crowds had disappeared, when the leaves were beginning to change colors and there was the hint of a chill in the air.

Like *O Pioneers!*, Cather's *My Ántonia* was very different from most other novels of that time. *My Ántonia* had no action, no form, no traditional love story. As Cather wrote later, "I decided that in writing it I would dwell very lightly on those things that a novelist would ordinarily emphasize, and make up my story of the little, every-day happenings and occurrences that form the greatest part of everyone's life and happiness."[5]

If anything, it is a love story for the prairie. The central character is a poor immigrant girl from Bohemia who speaks broken English and works for a family in town. Her character is based on a Bohemian girl Cather had known in Red Cloud, named Annie Pavelka Sadilek. Through the voice of Jim Burden, the narrator of Ántonia's story, Cather shared many of her own experiences growing up in Red Cloud.

Describing Annie Sadilek, Cather later wrote, "She was one of the truest artists I ever knew in the keenness and sensitiveness of her enjoyment, in her love of people and in her willingness to take pains."[6] Cather used such an unlikely character to represent

When she was a child in Nebraska, Cather met a Bohemian girl named Annie Pavelka Sadilek, pictured here at age seventeen. Annie was the model for Cather's main character in My Ántonia.

the enduring spirit of Nebraska and the people who settled there.

Houghton Mifflin published *My Ántonia* in the fall of 1918. It received rave reviews. One critic wrote that *My Ántonia* was "not only the best [work] done by Miss Cather, but also one of the best that any American has ever done."[7] Another important reviewer, Randolph Bourne, said that Cather "has taken herself out of the rank of provincial writers and given us something we can fairly class with the modern literary art the world over that is earnestly and richly interpreting the spirit of youth."[8] Like *O Pioneers!*, it was also considered an important addition to the best of American literature.

Although delighted with the reviews, Cather was disappointed when *My Ántonia* failed to become a best-seller. Still, she thought it was her best work yet. But Willa Cather was just getting started. The next ten years would become her busiest, with fame and honor just over the horizon.

Fame and Honor

Cather's next novel was inspired by World War I, which had raged in Europe since 1914. Cather grieved at the destruction of lives, property, and living conditions in so many of the places she had visited.

When the United States entered the war in 1917, many Americans were sent to fight. In May 1918, Cather learned that one of her cousins, G. P. Cather, had been killed in France while leading other soldiers in battle. That September, while Cather was visiting her family in Red Cloud, G. P.'s mother gave her his letters to read. As Cather was going through them, she thought of the idea for her next novel.

Cather worked on this next book, which would be

called *One of Ours*, for the next three years. During that time she spoke with many soldiers to learn about their war experiences. She also visited battlefields in France to see where her cousin had fought and died.

While working on *One of Ours*, however, Cather's disappointment with the low sales of *My Ántonia* continued. She began to wonder if her publisher, Houghton Mifflin, was doing enough to sell her books. Her dream of writing was being fulfilled, and her work was pleasing to herself, her readers, and her critics. Yet Cather was still struggling with money. She often had to put aside her novels to write articles that would pay her immediately so she could make ends meet. More book sales could solve that problem.

In the early spring of 1920, Cather made a bold move. She met with another publisher, Alfred A. Knopf. Mr. Knopf had begun his publishing company just five years earlier. His reputation had quickly built as that of a fresh newcomer to the publishing world. Cather also sensed that Knopf was more interested in publishing fine writing than in turning a quick profit. That was an attitude she liked.

Once Knopf and Cather had discussed their publishing goals, he offered to publish her books. She had mixed feelings about breaking her long ties with her friend Ferris Greenslet at Houghton Mifflin, but over time, Cather accepted. She later said, "I have always been proud that I asked young Mr. Knopf to take me over, with not so much as a hint from him that he would like to have me. It was a rather sudden decision. Did it work? The answer is, twenty years."[1]

With Knopf as her publisher, Cather's income increased greatly over time. She and Knopf also developed a warm friendship as they worked together. Their first project was called *Youth and the Bright Medusa*. Published in 1920, it was a collection of eight of Cather's short stories. Four had appeared earlier in *The Troll Garden*. The book was well received and sold steadily, thanks to Knopf's advertising.[2]

At the same time, Cather continued work on her latest novel, *One of Ours*. The main character, Claude Wheeler, was modeled after her cousin G. P. Cather. The story focuses on just six years of Claude's life. It describes his unhappiness at home on a Nebraska farm, his heroism as a soldier, and finally, his death in battle. As a backdrop to the story, Cather also included rich and expressive descriptions of Nebraska and France. Cather finished *One of Ours* in the late summer of 1921.

The next summer she discovered yet another retreat that was an ideal place for her to work. The heat in Red Cloud that summer had been particularly intense, and her mother had encouraged her to postpone her visit there. Instead, she and Edith Lewis went to Grand Manan, a Canadian island off the coast of Maine. It is a rugged, beautiful place—wild and heavily wooded. High cliffs form one side of the island; the other side slopes gently to the sea. To Cather, the island's natural beauty was unequaled.[3]

The living conditions on Grand Manan were quite primitive, with mail and most supplies brought in only twice a week by boat. Few people lived on the island, and Cather and Lewis rented a hundred-year-old cottage there called Orchardside. It was so rugged, it didn't even have electricity or indoor plumbing. But the women were used to living under rough conditions on their trips to the Southwest, and they were not bothered by the inconveniences. With its beauty and peacefulness, Grand Manan became the best place yet that Cather had found to write.

Cather was at Grand Manan when *One of Ours* was published by Knopf in August 1922. Reviews for *One of Ours* were mixed. Although many were positive, some critics complained that the story was unrealistic and too long. Yet the public loved it, and it quickly became a best-seller.

Cather also received hundreds of letters from soldiers telling her how much the book meant to them and how well it described their experiences.[4] Several years later she spoke of *One of Ours*, saying that of all her books, she liked the one best that "all the high brow critics knock. . . . I don't think it has as few faults perhaps as *My Ántonia* or *A Lost Lady*, but any story of youth, struggle and defeat can't be as smooth in outline and perfect in form as just a portrait."[5]

In 1923, Cather received the Pulitzer Prize for *One of Ours*. The Pulitzer Prize had been established in 1917 to award outstanding achievements in drama, literature, music, and journalism. It was, and still is today, one of the most prestigious honors an author can receive.

The sixth and next novel Cather wrote was *A Lost Lady*. It was based on still another person she had known in Red Cloud, Mrs. Lyra Garber. Mrs. Garber was the wife of Silas Garber, the man who had founded Red Cloud. As a girl Cather had always been fascinated with Mrs. Garber's charm and beauty. She decided to write about her when she learned of Mrs. Garber's death.

In an interview, Cather talked about Mrs. Garber as she had known her. She said:

> . . . A Lost Lady *was a woman I loved very much in my childhood. I wasn't interested in her character when I was little, but in her lovely hair and her laugh which made me happy clear down to my toes. . . . A* Lost Lady *was a beautiful ghost in my mind for twenty years before it came together as a possible subject for presentation. All the lovely emotions that one has had some day appear with bodies, and it isn't as if one found ideas suddenly. Before this the memories of these experiences and emotions have been like a perfume.*[6]

A Lost Lady is a short, simple story about the life of Marian Forrester and Niel Herbert, her young admirer. The book describes Forrester's slow decline, both physically and socially. Cather saw parallels between Mrs. Forrester's decline and the changes taking place on the Nebraska prairie. In Cather's opinion, progress in Nebraska had decreased the dignity and simplicity of life as she had known it there.

A Lost Lady was published in September 1923. It was considered by most critics to be Cather's finest work. As one reviewer said, "She has never done a better novel than *A Lost Lady* nor is she likely to. But then neither is any other writer of our day. This seems to us truly a great book."[7]

While the glowing reviews of *A Lost Lady* were still

fresh, Cather began work on her next novel, *The Professor's House*. She completed it in January 1925. The story takes place partly in the Mesa Verde area of Colorado and partly in a small Michigan town. The central character is a history professor named Godfrey St. Peter. He is modeled loosely on Cather herself. In the book, St. Peter has a successful career. Yet he becomes unhappy with his life and wonders what the future can hold for him. In the turning point of the book, the professor comes to terms with life's progression. He learns to face whatever the future holds.

In the spring of 1925, just after she finished *The Professor's House*, Cather wrote her eighth, and shortest, novel, *My Mortal Enemy*. Describing the life of its main character, Myra Henshawe, it is the bleakest of Cather's work. Myra dies at the end of the book, a poor, hopeless, and bitter woman.

After finishing *My Mortal Enemy*, Cather spent the summer of 1925 on another trip to the Southwest. She returned to New York in the fall, just after *The Professor's House* had been published. Cather was pleasantly surprised that the reviews were mainly favorable. She herself wrote in a letter that it was not her favorite work.[8] Several reviews, though, were negative. *The New York Times* called the book a "catastrophe," referring to parts as "amateurish" and "stale."[9]

My Mortal Enemy was published in 1926. The reviews were very mixed, with nearly half of them critical. The writing style Cather used in this book also drew disfavor. For years she had been working on a writing style in which she cut as much unnecessary detail as she could. In *My Mortal Enemy*, Cather's writing was unusually sparse. Commenting on that, one reviewer wrote, "Compression and selection grow naturally stronger in most good writers as they master their medium. But in *My Mortal Enemy* they have been carried too far. All bones and no flesh is never a wise method."[10]

With the completion of *My Mortal Enemy*, Cather ended a period of increasing bitterness and despair in her writing. Her next book, however, would turn in a more positive direction.

Cather's trip to the Southwest the previous summer had been especially fruitful. It was on that trip that the idea for her next novel emerged. As she wrote later:

> *The longer I stayed in the Southwest, the more I felt that the story of the Catholic Church in that country was the most interesting of all its stories. The old mission churches, even those which were abandoned and in ruins, had a moving reality about them; the hand-carved beams and joists, the utterly unconventional frescoes, the countless fanciful figures of the saints, not two of them alike, seemed a direct expression of some very real and lively human feeling. They were all fresh, individual, first-hand. Almost every one of those many remote little adobe churches in the mountains or in the desert had something lovely that was its own.*[11]

While in Santa Fe, New Mexico, she also read a book called *The Life of the Right Reverend Joseph P. Machebeuf*. It was written by a Catholic priest, Father William Howlett, and described the life and work of the first vicar general of the Roman Catholic Diocese of New Mexico.

All of Cather's powerful impressions about the American Southwest meshed with Howlett's story to form the basis of her next work. The historical novel that resulted describes the influence and contributions of the French missionaries in developing the southwestern frontier in the mid-1800s. Called *Death Comes for the Archbishop*, it is a story of simplicity, courage, and faith. The book ends with the archbishop's death and burial in the recently completed cathedral, after a life spent helping others.

About this book, Cather wrote:

> *I did not sit down to write the book until the feeling of it had so teased me that I could not get on with other things. The writing of it took only a few months, because the book had all been lived many times before it was written, and the happy mood in which I began it never paled. Writing this book was like a happy vacation from life, a return to childhood, to early memories.*[12]

Cather contentedly worked on *Death Comes for the Archbishop* through most of 1926. She spent the first half of 1927 reviewing her work before the book's publication. The summer of that year, however, brought an unsettling change to Cather's life. She was forced to leave the beloved apartment at 5 Bank Street that she and Edith Lewis had enjoyed for so long. The building was to be torn down and replaced with a newer apartment building. Their fifteen years on Bank Street had been Cather's happiest and most

This portrait shows Cather in 1926, when she wrote Death Comes for the Archbishop. *The book was extremely popular with the public and critics alike and won Cather many honors.*

successful, and the move upset them both. They reluctantly moved to the nearby Grosvenor Hotel on Fifth Avenue. At the time, they expected to stay there only a short while. Yet they ended up living at the Grosvenor for almost five years.

When *Death Comes for the Archbishop* was published in the fall of 1927, it became an overnight success. Bookstores couldn't keep enough copies of this novel, called an American classic, in stock. Said one reviewer, "It is not a tragic or a pathetic tale, but one full of happiness and triumph; and yet it moves one to tears, by the picture of such goodness and beauty seen through the medium of a faultless art."[13] With *Death Comes for the Archbishop*, Cather had the joy of seeing her work become a success with critics and the public.

By the end of 1927, Cather had written nine novels. She was a very successful author and known as one of the most prominent women in America. Money was no longer a concern for her. Her books had been translated into many languages and were sold all over the world. Sinclair Lewis, another famous American author, known especially for his best-selling novel *Main Street*, had praised Cather's work and called her Nebraska's leading citizen.[14] She had received honorary doctoral degrees from the universities of Nebraska and Michigan. She had also become a highly requested speaker and was flooded with requests for interviews by publications of all kinds.

Cather was indeed at the peak of her career. But just like her Professor St. Peter of *The Professor's House*, she also wondered what the future held.

Cather's Legacy

The publication of *Death Comes for the Archbishop* marked the end of Cather's busiest writing period. After that, she continued to write, but the normal changes and losses that occurred as she grew older left her distressed and sad.

In the spring of 1928, Cather's father died suddenly of a heart attack. This loss left her inconsolable. She had always felt close to her father, and his death was the first break in the circle of her immediate family. She returned to Red Cloud for his funeral and remained there for a month trying to cope with her loss.

Later that year Cather prepared to return to her beloved Grand Manan retreat. She took a different route to reach the island, however, this time traveling through Quebec, Canada. It was her first visit to that city, and its French history and culture reminded her of the France she had visited and loved earlier in her life. From Cather's brief visit to Quebec, she got the idea for her next novel, *Shadows on the Rock.*

Leaving Quebec, Cather and Lewis continued on to Grand Manan. Two years earlier Cather had bought property on the island and had arranged to have a cottage built there. By now, the cottage was completed. It stood on a hillside, surrounded by spruce and birch trees, about fifty yards from the edge of a cliff that overlooked a cove. Above the living room was a large attic with a view of the cliffs and the sea. The attic became Cather's study. There she continued her habit of writing for three hours each morning. Then she would walk along the cliffs to clear her mind and enjoy the wild beauty of the island.

Returning to New York in the fall, Cather worked on *Shadows on the Rock*, which she finished in 1930. In addition to completing *Shadows*, Cather was also honored that year by the American Academy of Arts and Letters, which presented her with the highly respected Howells Medal for *Death Comes for the Archbishop.* By this time she had also received honorary doctoral degrees from Creighton, Columbia, and Yale universities.

Shadows on the Rock was published in 1931. It is a historical novel based on life in Quebec in the 1690s. The story is about a young girl named Cecile and her friendships with a small boy, the nuns at her school, and a young trapper who opens up a world of adventure for her. Cather explained about the book in a letter:

> *I tried, as you say, to state the mood and the viewpoint in the title. To me the rock of Quebec is not only a stronghold on which many strange figures have for a little time cast a shadow in the sun; it is the curious endurance of a kind of culture, narrow but definite. There another age persists.*[1]

Incredibly popular with the public, *Shadows on the Rock* became the most widely read novel in the United States.[2] Despite the book's popular success, though, it received mixed reviews from critics. Most were favorable, but some criticized it as having no real story.[3]

Cather suffered another severe personal loss in 1931, with her mother's death. Now both of her parents were gone. Cather went back to Red Cloud for Christmas to see her brothers and sisters and to help take care of family affairs. After that, she never again returned to Red Cloud.

Despite the many losses in her personal life, the year 1931 continued to bring Cather increasing popularity and acclaim. Her picture was on the cover of *Time* magazine's August 3, 1931, issue, with its cover story about her success as a novelist. Also in 1931, she was named one of the Twelve Greatest American Women by *Good Housekeeping* magazine, and the University of California and Princeton University both awarded her with honorary doctoral degrees.

The next year Knopf published a collection of three of Cather's new short stories in a book called *Obscure Destinies*. One of the stories, called "Old Mrs. Harris,"

Willa Cather's novels sparked the imaginations of readers all around the world.

was considered by many critics to be the finest she had ever written. The central character is modeled after Cather's grandmother, Rachel Boak. Along with "Old Mrs. Harris," the book's other two stories are called "Neighbor Rosicky" and "Two Friends." All three stories were set in Nebraska once again, which pleased both readers and reviewers. Critics of *Obscure Destinies* were particularly positive about Cather's ability, once again, to make her readers care about the lives of ordinary people.[4]

Also in 1932, Cather and Lewis moved from the Grosvenor Hotel to an apartment at 570 Park Avenue. It would be Cather's last home. By this time, with all the attention that came with her fame, Cather treasured her privacy above all else. One of her friends described it this way:

> *A public figure through her own efforts, she stead-fastly refused to play the public figure, but lived a sedulously quiet life with her close friend and companion Edith Lewis in a Park Avenue apartment. Now and then she would be seen at concerts or the-ater, and now and then she would entertain a few guests . . . but most of the time she kept her distance from the world, and expected the world to keep its distance in return.*[5]

Yet Cather's celebrity continued. In 1933 she received the "Prix Femina Américain" for *Shadows on the Rock*. This French literary award was the first of its kind given to honor an American book translated into French. The same year she received still another honorary doctoral degree, this time from Smith College.

In August of 1935, Knopf published Cather's eleventh novel, *Lucy Gayheart*. It was about a girl who fails to fulfill her dream of becoming a concert pianist. In this book Cather again shows her love of music. She also continues her theme about the problems of expressing creativity while growing up in a small town. Although it was not considered her best work, most reviews for *Lucy Gayheart* were positive. It, too, became a best-seller.

The next year Knopf published a collection of six essays Cather had written, in a book called *Not Under Forty*. Then, in the spring of 1937, she began what would be her last novel, *Sapphira and the Slave Girl*. The story is set in the Shenandoah Valley of Virginia before the Civil War. It is about a slave named Nancy Till who escapes to freedom with the help of her owner's daughter. The events in the book are similar to a time in the Cather family when Grandmother Boak helped a slave escape across the Potomac River.

Cather would not finish *Sapphira and the Slave Girl* until the summer of 1940. She was interrupted in 1939 by two more devastating losses. One was the sudden death of her brother Douglass from a heart attack in June. The other was the long-expected death of her dearest friend, Isabelle McClung Hambourg, in October. Left completely bereft, Cather could not continue to write. She remained deeply depressed for months and did not resume working on *Sapphira and the Slave Girl* until the summer of 1939.

The book was published on Cather's birthday, December 7, 1940. Readers and critics alike loved this book, calling it one of her best. Four years later, all that Willa Cather had achieved as a writer was honored when she received the Gold Medal for Fiction from the National Institute of Arts and Letters.

On April 24, 1947, Willa Cather died unexpectedly of a cerebral hemorrhage at her Park Avenue home. She was seventy-four years old. She was buried in Jaffrey Center, New Hampshire, one of the writing places she had loved most. On her tombstone is a quotation from *My Ántonia:* " . . . that is happiness; to be dissolved into something complete and great." The

Willa Cather died on April 24, 1947, and was buried near her favorite writing place in Jaffrey, New Hampshire.

last three short stories she had written—"The Old Beauty," "Before Breakfast," and "The Best Years"— were published in 1948 in a book called *The Old Beauty and Others.*

In an interview years before she died, Cather spoke of her views about life. She said, "When people ask me if it has been a hard or easy road I always answer with the quotation, 'The end is nothing, the road is all.' " Explaining further, she said, "That is what I mean when I say my writing has been a pleasure. I have never faced the typewriter with the thought that one more chore had to be done."[6]

Cather's life was over. It had been a life of complete devotion to writing. Her work had been rewarded with success and fame, as well as a permanent place in history as one of the finest writers America has produced. Her spirit continues on in the many books she wrote that have deeply touched millions of readers.

Chronology

1873 — December 7, Willela Love Cather is born in Back Creek Valley, Virginia.

1874 — Cather family moves to Willow Shade, family home in Virginia.

1883 — Cather family moves to Webster County, Nebraska.

1884 — Cather family moves into the town of Red Cloud, Nebraska.

1890 — Willa graduates from high school in Red Cloud.

1891 — Enters the University of Nebraska, Lincoln; Cather's essay "The Personal Characteristics of Thomas Carlyle" is published in the *Nebraska State Journal*.

1895 — Cather graduates from University of Nebraska.

1896 — Moves to Pittsburgh to become editor of *Home Monthly* magazine.

1897 — Becomes telegraph editor of the *Pittsburgh Leader*.

1899 — Meets Isabelle McClung in Pittsburgh.

1901 — Teaches at Central High School in Pittsburgh; moves into McClung home.

1903 — First book, *April Twilights*, is published; begins teaching at Allegheny High School, Pittsburgh.

1905 — *The Troll Garden* is published.

1906 — Moves to New York City; becomes an editor of *McClure's Magazine*.

1908 — Becomes managing editor of *McClure's Magazine*; meets Sarah Orne Jewett.

1911 — Resigns from *McClure's Magazine*.

1912 — First novel, *Alexander's Bridge*, is published by Houghton Mifflin; makes first trip to Southwest.

1913 — *O Pioneers!* is published by Houghton Mifflin.

1915 — *The Song of the Lark* is published by Houghton Mifflin; first visit to cliff dwellings at Mesa Verde in Colorado.

1917 — Receives honorary doctorate from University of Nebraska; first visit to Shattuck Inn, Jaffrey, New Hampshire.

1918 — *My Ántonia* is published by Houghton Mifflin.

1920 — *Youth and the Bright Medusa* is published by Alfred A. Knopf.

1922 — *One of Ours* is published by Alfred A. Knopf; first visit to Grand Manan Island, New Brunswick, Canada.

1923 — Receives Pulitzer Prize for *One of Ours*; *A Lost Lady* is published by Alfred A. Knopf.

1924 — Receives honorary doctorate from University of Michigan.

1925 — *The Professor's House* is published by Alfred A. Knopf.

1926 — *My Mortal Enemy* is published by Alfred A. Knopf.

1927 — *Death Comes for the Archbishop* is published by Alfred A. Knopf.

1928 — Receives honorary doctorates from Creighton and Columbia universities; makes first visit to Quebec; father dies.

1929 — Elected to membership in National Institute of Arts and Letters; receives honorary doctorate from Yale University.

1930 — Receives Howells Medal for Fiction for *Death Comes for the Archbishop* from the American Academy of Arts and Letters.

1931— Receives honorary doctorates from the University of California and Princeton University; *Shadows on the Rock* is published by Alfred A. Knopf; mother dies.

1932— *Obscure Destinies* is published by Alfred A. Knopf.

1933— Receives Prix Femina Américain for *Shadows on the Rock*; receives honorary doctorate from Smith College.

1935— *Lucy Gayheart* is published by Alfred A. Knopf.

1936— *Not Under Forty* is published by Alfred A. Knopf.

1937— Houghton Mifflin begins publishing Autograph Edition of Cather's novels.

1938— Elected to membership in the American Academy of Arts and Letters; Isabelle McClung Hambourg dies.

1940— *Sapphira and the Slave Girl* is published by Alfred A. Knopf.

1944— Awarded National Institute of Arts and Letters Gold Medal for Fiction.

1947— Willa Cather dies on April 24; buried in Jaffrey Center, New Hampshire.

1948— *The Old Beauty and Others* is published by Alfred A. Knopf.

Books by Willa Cather

April Twilights, 1903

The Troll Garden, 1905

Alexander's Bridge, 1912

O Pioneers!, 1913

The Song of the Lark, 1915

My Ántonia, 1918

Youth and the Bright Medusa, 1920

One of Ours, 1922

A Lost Lady, 1923

The Professor's House, 1925

My Mortal Enemy, 1926

Death Comes for the Archbishop, 1927

Shadows on the Rock, 1931

Obscure Destinies, 1932

Lucy Gayheart, 1935

Not Under Forty, 1936

Sapphira and the Slave Girl, 1940

The Old Beauty and Others, 1948

Chapter Notes

Chapter 1. A Gold Medal

1. Phyllis C. Robinson, *Willa: The Life of Willa Cather* (Garden City, N.Y.: Doubleday, 1983), p. 186.

2. Willa Cather to S. S. McClure, May 26, 1944. Willa Cather's correspondence with S. S. McClure and his wife is in the Lilly Library at Indiana University, Bloomington, Indiana. Cited in Robinson, p. 3.

3. Robinson, p. 234.

4. Ann T. Keene, *Willa Cather* (New York: Simon and Schuster, 1994), p. 4.

Chapter 2. Southern Roots

1. Mildred R. Bennett, *The World of Willa Cather* (Lincoln: University of Nebraska Press, 1961), p. 26.

2. Edith Lewis, *Willa Cather Living* (New York: Alfred A. Knopf, 1953), p. 6.

3. Joan Acocella, "Cather and the Academy," *The New Yorker*, November 27, 1995, p. 58.

4. Lewis, p. 12.

5. Ibid., pp. 7–8.

Chapter 3. Transplanted to Nebraska

1. Interview in *Philadelphia Record*, August 10, 1913. Cited in L. Brent Bohlke, ed., *Willa Cather in Person* (Lincoln: University of Nebraska Press, 1986), p. 10.

2. Willa Cather, *My Ántonia* (Boston: Houghton Mifflin, 1918), p. 29.

3. *Philadelphia Record*, August 10, 1913. Cited in Bohlke, p. 10.

4. Mildred R. Bennett, *The World of Willa Cather* (Lincoln: University of Nebraska Press, 1961), p. xiii.

5. Bohlke, p. 10.

6. H. W. Boynton, "Chapters in 'The Great American Novel,'" New York *Evening Post*, November 13, 1915. Cited in Bennett, p. 169.

7. Bennett, p. 53.

8. Ibid, p. 13.

9. Lila Walz, "Bet You Didn't Know These Things About Nebraska," *Cobblestone*, December 1980, p. 23.

10. Bennett, p. 101.

11. *Omaha Daily Bee*, October 29, 1921. Cited in Bennett, p. 140.

12. Bennett, p. 112.

13. Interview by Eleanor Hinman, *Lincoln Sunday Star*, November 6, 1921. Cited in Bennett, p. 77.

14. Edith Lewis, *Willa Cather Living* (New York: Alfred A. Knopf, 1953), p. 30.

15. *Nebraska State Journal*, March 1, 1891. Cited in James Woodress, *Willa Cather: A Literary Life* (Lincoln: University of Nebraska Press, 1987), pp. 72–73.

16. Willa Cather, "One Way of Putting It," *Nebraska State Journal*, November 22, 1893. Cited in Bennett, p. 184.

17. Ann T. Keene, *Willa Cather* (New York: Simon and Schuster, 1994), p. 24.

Chapter 4. Opportunity in Pittsburgh

1. "City News," *The Red Cloud Chief*, June 26, 1896.

2. Phyllis C. Robinson, *Willa: The Life of Willa Cather* (Garden City, N.Y.: Doubleday, 1983), p. 80.

3. Willa Cather to Mariel Gere, April 27, 1897. Cited in James Woodress, *Willa Cather: A Literary Life* (Lincoln: University of Nebraska Press, 1987), p. 115.

4. Robinson, p. 88.

5. Dorothy Canfield Fisher, "Novelist Recalls Christmas in Blue-and-Gold Pittsburgh," *Chicago Tribune Magazine of Books*, December 21, 1947. Cited in Mildred R. Bennett, *The World of Willa Cather* (Lincoln: University of Nebraska Press, 1961), p. 121.

6. Robinson, p. 99.

7. Mildred R. Bennett, *The World of Willa Cather* (Lincoln: University of Nebraska Press, 1961), p. 192.

8. Willa Cather to Mariel Gere, April 25, 1897. Cited in Robinson, p. 93.

9. Interview by Flora Merrill, *New York World*, April 19, 1925, sec. 3, pp. 1, 6, cols. 1–5, 4–5. Cited in L. Brent Bohlke, ed., *Willa Cather in Person* (Lincoln: University of Nebraska Press, 1986), p. 76.

10. Phyllis Martin Hutchinson, "Reminiscences of Willa Cather as a Teacher," *Bulletin of the New York Public Library*, June 1956. Cited in Bohlke, p. 172.

11. James Woodress, *Willa Cather: A Literary Life* (Lincoln: University of Nebraska Press, 1987), pp. 153–154.

12. Merrill interview. Cited in Bennett, p. 150.

13. Edith Lewis, *Willa Cather Living* (New York: Alfred A. Knopf, 1953), p. 57.

14. Woodress, p. 170.

15. Ibid.

Chapter 5. The Spell of S. S. McClure

1. *Nebraska State Journal*, February 27, 1904. Cited in Mildred R. Bennett, *The World of Willa Cather* (Lincoln: University of Nebraska Press, 1961), p. 254.

2. Phyllis C. Robinson, *Willa: The Life of Willa Cather* (Garden City: Doubleday, 1983), p. 124.

3. Elizabeth Shepley Sergeant, *Willa Cather: A Memoir* (Philadelphia: J. B. Lippincott, 1953), p. 27.

4. Robinson, p. 121.

5. "People You Know," *Nebraska State Journal*, May 8, 1903. Cited in L. Brent Bohlke, ed., *Willa Cather in Person* (Lincoln: University of Nebraska Press, 1986), p. xxiii.

6. Charles Kingsley, *The Roman and the Teuton*. Cited in James Woodress, *Willa Cather: A Literary Life* (Lincoln: University of Nebraska Press, 1987), p. 172.

7. James Woodress, *Willa Cather, A Literary Life* (Lincoln: University of Nebraska Press, 1987), p. 173.

8. Bessie du Bois, *Bookman*, August 1905, pp. 612–614. Cited in Woodress, p. 179.

9. Interview by Eleanor Hinman, *Lincoln Sunday Star*, November 6, 1921. Cited in Mildred R. Bennett, *The World of Willa Cather* (Lincoln: University of Nebraska Press, 1961), p. 199.

10. Elizabeth Moorhead, *These Too Were Here: Louise Homer and Willa Cather*, p. 52. Cited in Bennett, p. 253.

11. Sergeant, p. 28.

12. Willa Cather, "Farewell to Students," June 6, 1906. Cited in Bohlke, p. 173.

13. Robinson, p. 155.

14. Sergeant, p. 47.

15. Ibid., p. 51.

Chapter 6. Boston Artists

1. Elizabeth Shepley Sergeant, *Willa Cather: A Memoir* (Philadelphia: J. B. Lippincott, 1953), p. 55.

2. L. Brent Bohlke, ed., *Willa Cather in Person* (Lincoln: University of Nebraska Press, 1986), p. 144.

3. Willa Cather, "148 Charles Street," *Not Under Forty* (New York: Alfred A. Knopf, 1936), p. 56.

4. Ibid., p. 58.

5. Sergeant, p. 41.

6. Cather, "148 Charles Street," p. 54.

7. Willa Cather, "Miss Jewett," *Not Under Forty* (New York: Alfred A. Knopf, 1936), p. 85.

8. Sarah Orne Jewett to Willa Cather, December 13, 1908, in *The Letters of Sarah Orne Jewett*, Annie Fields, ed. (Boston: Houghton Mifflin, 1911), pp. 247-250.

9. Edith Lewis, *Willa Cather Living* (New York: Alfred A. Knopf, 1953), p. 74.

10. Letters from Willa Cather to S. S. McClure; October 21, November 5, 17, 1911. Cited in James Woodress, *Willa Cather: A Literary Life* (Lincoln: University of Nebraska Press, 1987), p. 213.

11. James Woodress, *Willa Cather: A Literary Life* (Lincoln: University of Nebraska Press, 1987), p. 225.

12. Willa Cather, "My First Novels," *Willa Cather on Writing* (New York: Alfred A. Knopf, 1949), pp. 92–93.

13. Interview by Eva Mahoney, Omaha *Sunday World-Herald*, November 27, 1921. Cited in Mildred R. Bennett, *The World of Willa Cather* (Lincoln: University of Nebraska Press, 1961), p. 199.

14. Cather, "My First Novels," pp. 92–93.

15. Ibid., p. 93.

16. Phyllis C. Robinson, *Willa: The Life of Willa Cather* (Garden City. N.Y.: Doubleday, 1983), pp. 182–183.

17. Lewis, p. 17.

18. Mahoney interview. Cited in Bennett, pp. 194–195.

Chapter 7. The Allure of the West

1. Phyllis C. Robinson, *Willa: The Life of Willa Cather* (Garden City, N.Y.: Doubleday, 1983), p. 173.

2. Elizabeth Shepley Sergeant, *Willa Cather: A Memoir* (Philadelphia: J. B. Lippincott, 1953), pp. 79–80.

3. Edith Lewis, *Willa Cather Living* (New York: Alfred A. Knopf, 1953), pp. 80–81.

4. Sergeant, p. 82.

5. Lucia Woods and Bernice Slote, *Willa Cather: A Pictorial Memoir* (Lincoln: University of Nebraska Press, 1973), p. 57.

6. Interview by Eva Mahoney, *Omaha Sunday World-Herald*, November 27, 1921. Cited in Mildred R. Bennett, *The World of Willa Cather* (Lincoln: University of Nebraska Press, 1961), p. 139.

7. Robinson, p. 186.

8. Ibid., p. 185.

9. Willa Cather, "My First Novels," *Willa Cather on Writing* (New York: Alfred A. Knopf, 1949), p. 94.

10. Robinson, p. 186.

11. Lewis, p. 85.

12. Cather, "My First Novels," p. 96.

Chapter 8. A Single Purpose

1. Edith Lewis, *Willa Cather Living* (New York: Alfred A. Knopf, 1953), p. 96.

2. Willa Cather, *The Professor's House* (New York: Alfred A. Knopf, 1925), p. 202.

3. Phyllis C. Robinson, *Willa: The Life of Willa Cather* (Garden City, N.Y.: Doubleday, 1983), p. 209.

4. Interview by Eleanor Hinman, *Lincoln Sunday Star*, November 6, 1921. Cited in Mildred R. Bennett, *The World of Willa Cather* (Lincoln: University of Nebraska Press, 1961), p. 76.

5. Hinman interview. Cited by L. Brent Bohlke, ed., *Willa Cather in Person* (Lincoln: University of Nebraska Press, 1986), pp. 44–45.

6. Ibid., p. 44.

7. James Woodress, *Willa Cather: A Literary Life* (Lincoln: University of Nebraska Press, 1987), p. 301.

8. Ibid.

Chapter 9. Fame and Honor

1. Edith Lewis, *Willa Cather Living* (New York: Alfred A. Knopf, 1953), p. 115.

2. James Woodress, *Willa Cather: A Literary Life* (Lincoln: University of Nebraska Press, 1987), p. 310.

3. Lewis, p. 128.

4. Ibid., p. 123.

5. Interview by Flora Merrill, *New York World*, April 19, 1925, sec. 3, 1:2.

6. Merrill interview.

7. Woodress, p. 351.

8. Willa Cather to Dorothy Canfield Fisher, February 27, 1925. Cited in Woodress, p. 366.

9. Woodress, p. 376.

10. Ibid., p. 388.

11. Willa Cather, "On *Death Comes for the Archbishop*," *Willa Cather on Writing* (New York: Alfred A. Knopf, 1949), p. 5.

12. Ibid., pp. 10–11.

13. Woodress, p. 410.

14. *Omaha Morning World-Herald*, April 9, 1921. Cited in Woodress, p. 319.

Chapter 10. Cather's Legacy

1. Willa Cather, "On *Shadows on the Rock*," *Willa Cather on Writing* (New York: Alfred A. Knopf, 1949), p. 15.

2. Joan Acocella, "Cather and the Academy," *The New Yorker*, November 27, 1995, p. 63.

3. James Woodress, *Willa Cather: A Literary Life* (Lincoln: University of Nebraska Press, 1987), p. 433.

4. Ann T. Keene, *Willa Cather* (New York: Simon and Schuster, 1994), p. 108.

5. Fannie Butcher, "Three Long Short Stories by Willa Cather," *Chicago Daily Tribune*, October 12, 1948, p. 3. Cited in L. Brent Bohlke, ed., *Willa Cather in Person* (Lincoln: University of Nebraska Press, 1986), p. xxviii.

6. Interview by Flora Merrill, *New York World*, April 19, 1925, sec. 3, 1:2.

Further Reading

Bennett, Mildred R. *The World of Willa Cather*. Lincoln: University of Nebraska Press, 1961.

Bohlke, L. Brent, ed. *Willa Cather in Person*. Lincoln: University of Nebraska Press, 1986.

Keene, Ann T. *Willa Cather*. New York: Simon and Schuster, 1994.

Lewis, Edith. *Willa Cather Living*. New York: Alfred A. Knopf, 1953.

Robinson, Phyllis C. *Willa, the Life of Willa Cather*. Garden City, N.Y.: Doubleday, 1983.

Sergeant, Elizabeth Shepley. *Willa Cather, A Memoir*. Philadelphia: J. B. Lippincott, 1953.

Woodress, James. *Willa Cather, A Literary Life*. Lincoln: University of Nebraska Press, 1987.

Woods, Lucia, and Bernice Slote. *Willa Cather, A Pictorial Memoir*. Lincoln: University of Nebraska Press, 1973.

Index